D1226698

DOROTHEA LANGE

DOROTHEA LANGE

A VISUAL LIFE

Edited by

ELIZABETH PARTRIDGE

SMITHSONIAN INSTITUTION PRESS

WASHINGTON AND LONDON

Editor: Catherine F. McKenzie
Production Editor: Jack Kirshbaum
Designer: Kathleen Sims
Production Manager: Ken Sabol

Library of Congress Cataloging-in-Publication Data

Dorothea Lange—a visual life / edited by Elizabeth Partridge.
Includes bibliographical references.
ISBN 1-56098-350-7 (alk. paper).
—ISBN 1-56098-455-4 (pbk. alk. paper)
1. Lange, Dorothea.   2. Women photographers—United States—
Biography.   I. Lange, Dorothea.   II. Partridge, Elizabeth.
III. Title: Visual life.
TR140.L3D67   1994
770'.92—dc1994
770'.93—dc20
[B]   94-25689

British Library Cataloging-in-Publication Data available

Printed in the United Kingdom by Balding and Mansell
98 97 96 95 94 5 4 3 2 1

∞The paper used in this publication meets the minimum requirements of the American
National Standard for Permanence of Paper for Printed Library Materials Z39.48–1.

For permission to reproduce any of the illustrations, please correspond directly with the sources.
The Smithsonian Institution Press does not retain reproduction rights for these illustrations
individually or maintain a file of addresses for photo sources.

Cover illustrations
Front: Dorothea Lange, 1936, by Rondal Partridge. Private collection
Back: Migrant Agricultural Worker in Marysville, California, Migrant Camp Trying to Figure
Out His Year's Earnings, October 1935, by Dorothea Lange. U.S. Farm Security Administration,
Prints and Photographic Division, Library of Congress

Front matter illustrations
Frontispiece: Dorothea with Zeiss Juwel Camera, 1937, by Rondal Partridge. Private collection
Opposite epigraph: Dorothea with Graflex, 1937, by Rondal Partridge. Private collection
Opposite contents: "You Ain't Looking Fer Money, Is You?" by Dorothea Lange, North
Carolina, July 4, 1939. U.S. Farm Security Administration, Prints and Photographic Division,
Library of Congress

The companion film, *Dorothea Lange: A Visual Life,* is available from Pacific Pictures,
P.O. Box 305, Valley Ford, CA 94972-0305, (800) 886–3135.

In memory of
Paul Schuster Taylor
and
his beloved
New Deal

One should really use the camera as though tomorrow you'd be stricken blind.
To live a visual life is an enormous undertaking, practically unattainable. I have only touched it, just touched it.

—*Dorothea Lange*

CONTENTS

ACKNOWLEDGMENTS

I am deeply indebted to those who had the foresight to record Dorothea Lange's words while she was still alive: Suzanne Riess of the Regional Oral History Office at the University of California; the KQED Film Unit, comprising Phillip Greene, Robert Katz, and Richard Moore, who made two films about Lange, *Closer for Me* and *Under the Trees,* and, using an "open mike," captured more than thirty hours of Dorothea talking; and Richard Doud, who interviewed Dorothea for the Archives of American Art.

I am grateful to my sister Meg Partridge, who directed this book's companion film, *Dorothea Lange: A Visual Life.* I also received help from my sister Joan Partridge and my friends Linda Glaser and Kay McArthur, editors extraordinaire.

Many of the images in this book were printed by my father, Ron Partridge. As I worked on the book, he taught me to "see" the fullness of Dorothea's photos. He encouraged me when I lagged, and told me story after story about Dorothea, all of which he swore were true.

The greater Dixon-Taylor-Lange clan was always helpful, particularly Helen, Dan, and John Dixon, Dyanna Taylor, and Christina Gardner. They dragged old photographs of Dorothea's out from under beds and off closet shelves, and never tired of my many questions.

The staff at the Oakland Museum, led by Therese Heyman, were unfailingly cooperative with the research and reproduction work I compiled from the Dorothea Lange Collection. Drew Johnson and Janice Capecci were sterling.

The scholars Roger Daniels, Dan Dixon, Clark Kerr (and his secretary, Maureen Kawaoka), Linda Morris, and Sally Stein brought a wide expertise to this book. They were always generous with their time and knowledge, not only in writing their essays but in teaching me what they knew.

And pulling all this together with grace and skill was my editor at the Smithsonian Institution Press, Amy Pastan, who was always a great delight to work with.

1

Elizabeth Partridge

INTRODUCTION

I was fourteen when Dorothea died. Up to that moment I had taken her presence in my life for granted. I knew her as the head of a complicated family made up of her children, stepchildren, and grandchildren, with my family stuck fast to the edges. She stood central in all of our lives, with an incontestable will. Driven by a fiercely self-critical nature, she pushed herself to photograph as she did, often at great personal cost. She held her extended family closely, sometimes to the detriment of family members. As a child I was held tightly by these powerful bonds, but it has taken me many years as an adult to understand Dorothea's complexity and the depth of her relationships.

My father's mother was Imogen Cunningham, a San Francisco photographer. "We were very good friends," said Dorothea of my grandmother. "What we call family friends, you know."[1] When my father, Ron, decided he wanted to be a photographer, his mother taught him all she knew, then sent him to be apprenticed to Dorothea.

As a teenager Ron drove Dorothea up and down California. He developed her negatives and made her prints. All the while, he was watching, learning, and taking his own photographs side by side with Dorothea. Slightly older than Dorothea's two children and three stepchildren, Ron was gradually drawn into the family, almost as a son. When he married my mother at twenty-three and they had their first child, Joan, Dorothea designated Joan her goddaughter as a way to honor the bond. One by one the rest of us Partridge children entered this group, family and yet not quite family.

Though a source of bittersweet grief and struggle to her grown children, Dorothea was the bringer of magic to the rest of us. This was particularly evident during the holidays, when our families gathered together [1.1]. I clearly remember back to a Christmas when I was six years old.

Dusk was already settling over Berkeley as we wound our way down the long brick pathway to Paul and Dorothea's house. Candles set in white paper bags flickered on both sides of the path. My loose-jointed father went first, then we four kids, bundled in big coats against the cold. At the end of the procession came my mother, stepping carefully on the rain-dampened bricks.

Dorothea stood waiting in the arched wooden doorway. Her short-cropped hair cradled her head like a soft gray cap. She wore a white peasant blouse with full gathered sleeves, and a dark blue homespun cotton skirt reaching nearly to the floor. Silver Navaho beads glimmered around her neck. From behind Dorothea, golden light flooded out of the house, reflecting softly on the wet bricks and shiny tree leaves.

"Partridges!" she called out affectionately. "You're late!" My father threw his arms open wide. "As always, Dorrie." Dorothea reached up to hug my father. Shy and full of

1.1.   Meg Partridge and Dorothea Lange, Christmas 1960, by Ron Partridge. Collection of Rondal Partridge.

expectation, I stood, waiting. Dorrie slid her hand onto the crown of my head and smiled down into my eyes, welcoming me in. I slipped past her into the warmth and smells of Christmas.

Paul was just emerging from the kitchen carrying the huge Christmas ham. Impatiently I danced on tiptoe next to him until he set down the ham and caught me up in his arms. I squeezed him back, hard, as Dorothea rang the dinner gong. Paul stood as the ceremonial head of the meal, cutting the ham and placing a huge piece on each thick terra-cotta plate. But we all knew Dorothea was really in charge, instructing the women to pile our plates with homemade rolls and cranberry sauce, buttery mashed potatoes, yams, green beans, and creamed onions, with a big spoonful of dark green salad squeezed onto one side.

Carefully steadying my plate, I took my dinner to the living room and perched on a stool next to the fire. Dorothea's son John, with a tense, muscular body hiding his tender heart, sat on the couch. His two boys, Andy and Gregor, wriggled onto the couch on either side of him. Dorothea's older son Dan, bright and sarcastic, took a chair next to the fireplace. Ross, Dorothea's stepson, sat in an overstuffed chair with his five-year-old daughter, Dee. One by one, other grandchildren and men came in. At last, when the serving was done, the women joined the group.

As I ate, I looked carefully over at the far wall. That long white expanse was Dorothea's work space. Every time we went to the house, new photographs were up on the wall, silver pushpins carefully holding down all four corners.

"These few feet of wall are in constant use by me," Dorothea frequently remarked. "Sometimes I have my own things there, sometimes I have things I have discovered of other people's that I like to look at. Those things that I put out there are for me to study, to evaluate, to accept, to discard, to unify, to absorb."[2]

But for Christmas she took all the work down and put up holiday mementos. There was a letter to Santa, written in the thirties, next to a photo of her son Dan, mouth wide open, singing heartily. There was a letter from Paul, with a V for victory across the top, celebrating Dorothea's release from the hospital following months of medical care.

After dinner the unmistakable sound of bells came from outside. "I don't think Santa can get down the chimney with the fire burning," Dorothea said. "Maybe he'll need the window." As she unlocked the floor to ceiling window, a red arm shot out of the night and pulled the window open. "Ho-ho-ho," said Santa, and then he was in, settled in the middle of the room, his fat sack bulging on the floor, a string of yak bells tossed to one side. One by one, we encircled him, just an arm's length away.

Santa settled a pair of glasses on his nose, black ones just like Paul's, and pulled the first present out of the bag. "Andy," he said, in a deep ringing voice. "Where's Andy?" Three-year-old Andy turned and bolted for his father, burying his face in John's neck. From hand to hand, the present was passed back to him.

Santa peered at the next present. "Where's Bitsie?" Strangely, my feet refused to move forward. "Go on!" said Dee, giving me a shove in the middle of my back. I lurched forward and caught my balance, hands outstretched for the little package Santa was holding out to me. "Thank you," I whispered, stepping back into the circle.

Inside the Japanese wrapping paper was a small, cream-covered picture book, *Charlotte and the White Horse,* illustrated by Maurice Sendak. With one finger, I eased open the cover. Inside was written, "A book for Bitsie, from Dorrie." I looked up in astonishment and searched for Dorothea. She was sitting on the stairs next to my father. How had she ever found Santa to give him the book?

Dorothea smiled at me, the laugh lines fanning out from her eyes in long, whirling crescents. "Merry Christmas," she said softly, her voice weaving through the laughter.

Summers we often went to Steep Ravine. There, in Paul and Dorothea's little cabin perched on a cliff hanging over the Pacific Ocean, we shed most of our clothes, and all sense of time. We had nothing but the vastness of the ocean and a tiny shell of a cabin, which cradled us all gently when the sun and wind wore us out [1.2].

Here Dorothea walked slowly through the wet sand, the wind blowing in off the ocean, the ever-present Pentax camera hanging from her neck. Inside the cabin she hung her camera on a nail by the door, ready to take photographs indoors or out. Here the worries that tugged perpetually at adults didn't seem to bother them, and we kids ate and quarreled and slept happily together like a litter of puppies.

It was at Steep Ravine that I began to see the interplay between Dorothea and Paul. Paul adored Dorothea with a steady fervor that brooked no defiance. Dorothea's mercurial and intense nature found solace in his unending romantic devotion. "Paul," she said simply, "is my rock."

Paul was slow moving and thoughtful; it was easy to underestimate the strength of his convictions. Like Jefferson, he believed fervently in an agrarian democracy. His beliefs sustained him, and nourished Dorothea. A professor of economics at the University of California at Berkeley, he loved teaching and debating. Surrounded by the noise and playfulness of the family, Paul would sit quietly in the main room of the cabin, patient as a fisherman. Only the flush of his cheeks showed his excitement.

"Bitsie," he called gently, as I ran past one day on the heels of Gregor and Dee. He called again, just a little bit louder. Gregor looked back at me and almost laughed, but in his eyes was a look of relief that it was I, not he, who was called.

"What do you think?" Paul asked, as I dropped into the seat facing his. This was his entreaty to tell him my opinions on such faraway subjects as politics and agrarian reform and water rights for farmers. Only ten, I was not nearly as interested as he thought I should be. "About what?" I asked, dodging. "How about Adlai Stevenson's speech last week," he prompted. I struggled with myself a moment, caught between talking with Paul and playing with Dee and Gregor. "I didn't hear it," I admitted.

Paul's cheeks flushed up a brighter red. I wasn't going to settle in for a talk, and he knew it. "The trouble with you kids today," he said firmly, "is you don't know anything about the New Deal." It was a self-defeating phrase, precisely because of its accuracy. I didn't know anything about the New Deal. As far as I could tell, the New Deal was very old. I smiled apologetically and ran off to join Dee and Gregor.

Thanksgiving and Christmas became more complicated as I grew older. I began to feel the undercurrents of tension running through the magic. In the kitchen, as the women

1.2.   Dorothea and Imogen at Steep Ravine, 1962, by Ron Partridge. (Author is in foreground in pigtails.) Collection of Rondal Partridge.

basted the turkey and unmolded the cranberry salad, they spoke in hushed, fragmented whispers of their difficulties with Dorothea. They told stories of Dorothea's iron will pressing into the fabric of their married lives. There was a feeling of their bitter-tasting obedience as they came up, again and again, against her unyielding nature.

In some mysterious way it made me cautious of Dorothea. I began to keep a small distance from her so that I would not find bitterness in my heart as the women did. Dee, stubborn and courageous, was the only one of us kids who would stand up to Dorothea.

Once, smelling distress on the air, I rounded the top of the stairs to discover Dee, flushed and tear-streaked, staring angrily at her mother, Onnie. "Why does Grandma Dorrie hate me?" Dee rubbed at the strands of fine blonde hair stuck to her moist face. "Oh, Dee, she doesn't hate you," said her mother. "It's just that you're both so strong-willed." I turned and fled downstairs. I was made of softer stuff.

In 1964 Dorothea was diagnosed with an incurable cancer of the esophagus. She decided to use her last months to put together a retrospective at the Museum of Modern Art and to let a television crew film her working on the show.

There was a sudden shift in the mood at Paul and Dorothea's house. Carefully, Dorothea used her last resources to choose the prints for the show. She drank cup after cup of tea and ate tiny bowls of polenta and ice cream. Up onto the long white wall went groups of photos, while she searched for the prints and combinations that would please her [1.3, 1.4]. "In this show, I would like to be speaking to others in the sound of my own voice, poor though it may be. Not other people's voices. I don't care how wide I lay myself open this time."[3]

A few weeks after choosing the final photographs for her show, Dorothea died. Paul, in an effort to console us, himself inconsolable, wrote down her very last words. "Isn't it a miracle," Dorothea said, "that it comes at the right time."[4] In the final moment, after a lifetime of striving, Dorothea met her own death and surrendered graciously.

Something gave way in me at Dorothea's memorial. As she had made childhood magic for me at Christmas, her death now tore that magic away. I understood, with the irrevocable clarity of a teenager, there is an end to those whose lives are woven together with ours.

Recently my father was asked to speak with Dorothea's son John at an exhibition of her photography at the Oakland Museum. My father talked about Dorothea's photographic technique and what she saw and taught him to see. He talked of her restless urgency, how they would stay out on the streets shooting all day, after which she would send him into the darkroom in the evening to develop the day's work. Some nights he would finish so late that the streetcars were no longer running, and he would curl up in the dry leaves in the yard and sleep like a cat.

John spoke quietly, reaching way back for childhood memories of his mother. He told all of us about the vast house he lived in when he was little, with his mother's darkroom upstairs, far down a dark hall. He spoke briefly of being boarded with other

1.3.   Dorothea Lange at Home Working on the MOMA Show, 1964, by Ron
Partridge. Collection of Rondal Partridge.

1.4.   Dorothea Lange at Home Working on the MOMA Show, 1964, by Ron
Partridge. Collection of Rondal Partridge.

families, starting when he was three, so that Dorothea could go on long photography trips. He talked about his mother photographing a fistful of daisies he once offered her, rather than taking him into her arms. And always, as far back as he could remember, her hands smelled of chemicals from the darkroom.

John told us how in his adulthood he brought his new babies home from the hospital and offered them to his mother's camera, just as he had offered her the daisies years before. This was the mother he remembered, who saved the best part of herself for her work. And by inference mostly, but also by the pain that chased across his eyes as he spoke, he let us see that he wished he'd had a little more. Yet he was proud of his mother, proud of her strength and driven nature. "Not good enough, Dorothea," she often said while looking at her photographs. "I remember her saying that, over and over," John remarked. "She said it all her life. 'Not good enough, Dorothea.'"

After the talk came questions from the audience, and in the pause just before the session ended, a man rose to his feet at the back of the room and asked my father, "Ron, why did you work for Dorothea, and not your mother, Imogen?"

Ron held up his hand, fingers splayed out. "Dorothea fed me," he said, folding down his little finger with his other hand. "She paid me a dollar a week." He folded down his ring finger. He stopped, puzzling out how to go on. "You're forgetting something, Ron," said John, leaning back against the side wall. "She loved you." Ron folded down his third finger. "Yes. She loved me." He smiled, a tender, sad smile rich with longing. "And I loved her," he said gently, dropping his hands.

Like many others whose lives were touched by Dorothea, I have found that death has not ended my relationship with her. I often see photographs she would have liked, moments she would have photographed. I am drawn to her contradictions—a woman who left her own children time and again, yet returned, gracious and full of magic, to her grandchildren; a woman who fought for personal and artistic freedom, yet constrained her own children and their spouses. Rather than fading over time, the pull of Dorothea's presence has become more insistent.

A few years ago I decided to put together this book on Dorothea's photography. Working on the book, I have lived with her proof sheets and photos, her journals, letters, and interviews. During this time, which has been like an apprenticeship for me, I have come to know Dorothea as a photographer as well as the family matriarch. I have stretched myself to see what she saw, and laughed and wept over her poignancy. I have felt the intense joy and despair she found in life and captured in her photographs.

During these last two years, I have begun to see more clearly and to feel more deeply than before. I have learned to hold tenaciously to my own creative path, despite the difficulties. And I have found Dorothea's photography so vibrant, so full of her essence, that I am hopeful her work can inspire others as well.

1. Dorothea Lange, *The Making of a Documentary Photographer,* an oral history interview conducted in 1960 and 1961 by Suzanne Riess (Berkeley: Regional Oral History Office, Bancroft Library, University of California, Berkeley, 1968), p. 107.

2. Outtakes from the interviews of Dorothea Lange, 1963–1965, held in her home at 1163 Euclid Avenue, Berkeley, Calif., for two films produced for National Educational Television by KQED, Inc., San Francisco (*Closer for Me* and *Under the Trees),* tape 13, p. 282. Copyright and all other rights held by Dorothea Lange Collection, The Oakland Museum, gift courtesy of Robert Katz and Paul Schuster Taylor.

3. Outtakes, tape 6, p. 120.

4. Paul Schuster Taylor in an open letter to the family, n.d., in the possession of John Dixon.

2

Linda A. Morris

A WOMAN OF OUR GENERATION

We need to be reminded these days about what women have been and can be, it's a question of their place in society. The really deep and fundamental place in society.

—Dorothea Lange, ca. 1964

As her photography reveals, Dorothea Lange had tremendous respect for the people she photographed, with special empathy for the women whose "deep and fundamental place in society" she celebrated. Yet Lange's own life differed sharply in a number of ways from the lives of the women she photographed. She aggressively pursued photography as a career, often putting her work before her family, before her children. Frequently that work took her away from her home, away from her friends and family, and put her on the road, often alone, among strangers. Instead of occupying a "deep and fundamental place," she was a pioneer who seized the opportunities that were presented to her. Above all else, she was a highly productive professional woman.

In her photography, Dorothea Lange saw the inner strength in people who were pushed to their own personal limits. Even when she photographed men and women in desperate economic, social, and emotional circumstances, she captured their innate human dignity. She also saw in her subjects what she called "courage, real courage. Undeniable courage. . . . I encountered that, many times, in unexpected places. And I have learned to recognize it when I see it."[1] These characteristics play an important part in her work because they were traits Lange shared with those she photographed. But unlike her subjects, she was a powerful and focused professional photographer who drove herself to the point of exhaustion and collapse and who for many years committed all her talents to issues of social justice.

Not so clearly reflected in her photography is the fact that she had to overcome considerable obstacles to achieve her greatness. Disabled as a young girl by polio, she considered herself "crippled" by the limp that was the visible legacy of the disease; she carried its deeper scars internally. In later life she was debilitated by serious, extended bouts of ulcers and esophagitis, and called upon deep inner strengths to combat these physical limitations. Even in the final year of her life, when she was diagnosed with inoperable, incurable cancer of the esophagus, she marshaled her strength and determination to prepare a retrospective of her work for the Museum of Modern Art in New York and to publish her final collection of photographs, entitled *Dorothea Lange Looks at the American Country Woman.*

Lange was equally unwilling to give in to other kinds of limitations imposed upon her. As a mother, she made very difficult, unpopular choices about her work and about her family—choices that had profound personal effects on her two sons and, in time, her stepchildren. Her work came first. As her assistant Ron Partridge later observed, she never considered giving up even five years of her life for her boys: "It didn't approach her mentality." Yet the choices she made also caused her considerable personal pain. As another assistant understood, "she knew the importance of maternity, but wasn't [herself] a very maternal person."[2] Those who have commented on her life and work have judged her harshly for making her work her priority. In our time, however, her effectiveness as a mother is no standard by which to judge her or to understand her. As she said of one of her own colleagues: "But when anyone asks me what do I know about someone who's an artist, I can only answer, 'Please, look at his work.' Because if you want to know anything about a person, doesn't his work tell you? I mean, how can you know more?"[3]

While the individual in the quote above refers specifically to a male colleague, Walker Evans, Dorothea Lange in fact had no way to think of herself as a woman *and* a photographer. In referring to herself professionally, she only employed the masculine pronouns "he" and "him." For example, in asking for her own set of proofs from undeveloped film she had sent to Washington, she argued that a photographer needed "to have some sort of a record of what *he* has been doing. It guides *him* in how the work is building up, whether or not it is taking form. Without this a photographer away from the office is lost because *he* forgets."[4]

Even some of her friends and colleagues, such as Ansel Adams, judged her to be a difficult woman.[5] She was indeed opinionated, impatient, and willful. Ultimately, the extent to which she defied traditional gender expectations caused Roy Stryker to dismiss her from the Farm Security Administration for being "uncooperative." If she sensed how some people perceived her, she never wavered in her determination. As a woman moving in a man's world, a photographer working in uncharted territory, Lange was repeatedly called upon to make nontraditional choices; it was the only way to meet the challenges posed by the unprecedented social and economic upheavals of the Great Depression. She was equal to the challenge, but at great personal cost.

In this regard, she identified directly with some of the women she photographed, those she called "modern" women. In preparing a section focusing on women for her retrospective show, she called her interviewer's attention to two photographs she felt were needed to complete her celebration of women's life: "I found I didn't have any modern women, and so I went back and I found my stenog at that lunch counter. And I also found the other woman, do you see her? The one who's holding a man's job? You see her? She with the stresses and the strains? See her? *That's a woman of our generation.*"[6]

In addition to her remarkable drive and determination, chance helped bring her to the threshold of her greatness. Nothing in her family background suggests that she would become one of the key architects in shaping our vision of the human costs of the Dust Bowl and the Depression; as she said when she began photographing migrant farm workers, she didn't know a tractor from a mule. Nor could anyone have foreseen that the artistry she developed in her portrait studio would enable her to create vivid representations of the uprooted farm families that poured into California in the 1930s. When the effects of the Depression first were felt in San Francisco, she was drawn out onto the streets with her camera, though she had no idea what she could do with the photographs she produced. Only the most fortuitous coincidence brought them to the attention of the Berkeley social scientist Paul Taylor, who ultimately became her husband and her collaborator. Lange later acknowledged that "Maynard [Dixon, Lange's first husband] and the FSA were my teachers; Paul opened doors for me and was my guide."[7] But Lange brought to her work her own passionate sense of social justice. She identified with the people she saw pushed to the edge by circumstances, and found in them heroic courage and dignity.

Although Dorothea Lange is best known for her photographs taken during the Depression, she continued to work for nearly three decades on a wide range of subjects, from the internment of Japanese Americans in Manzanar to the quiet, personal moments in her grandchildren's lives. When her health permitted, she went into the field on assignment for magazines such as *Life*, photographing Mormon communities in Utah, shipbuilders in Richmond, California, and families in Ireland. She traveled with Taylor to Asia, South America, Egypt, and India, taking photographs whenever and wherever she could, and becoming frustrated when she could not. When her health was compromised, she still continued to shoot pictures but, of necessity, closer to home. Even when she was housebound, her camera was never far from her reach. From the perspective of her grandchildren, it was as familiar a part of her as the heavy silver ring and bracelet she always wore. Dorothea Lange was first and foremost a photographer; it was her identity, her passion, her life.

Dorothea Lange was born in 1895 in Hoboken, New Jersey, the first child of Joan Lange and Henry Nutzhorn, both first-generation German immigrants. A second child, Henry, was born when Dorothea was six. When she was seven, she contracted polio, which left her with a withered right lower leg and a noticeable limp. Lange saw it as a determinative factor in her life, one that shaped her very personality, and one from which she could never escape.[8] Even if in later years her limp might have been an asset that helped make strangers more receptive to her when she was photographing in the field, there was no question that being partially "crippled," as she put it, posed a great personal challenge.

In 1907, when Dorothea was twelve, her father abandoned his family, and she and her mother and brother moved in with her maternal grandmother, Sophie Lange, in whose New Jersey house they lived until Dorothea left home at the age of twenty-three. The relationships between the three generations of Lange women were complicated at best. According to Lange, her mother was overly dependent on her daughter and overly impressed with other people's opinions. She felt self-conscious about Dorothea's limp and admonished her to try to walk more normally, which predictably deepened her daughter's self-consciousness. "She was [also] slightly obsequious to anyone in authority. . . . I never liked it at all. . . . She was also rather sentimental, which I have been too, but I loathe it in other people."[9] The affinity between Dorothea and her grandmother was stronger, but her grandmother was an alcoholic and, according to Lange, tyrannical.

When her mother began to commute to a job in the New York Public Library in lower Manhattan, she enrolled Dorothea in a public school in the lower East Side, where she was the only gentile among all Jewish children. Not being from the neighborhood and feeling isolated culturally, Dorothea led a relatively lonely existence as a schoolgirl. In retrospect, the best she could report of her childhood was that her family mostly let her alone. Her high school years were a slight improvement when she transferred to a girls' school in upper Manhattan. When pressed by her family at graduation to declare what work she intended to do, Dorothea announced that she was going to become a photographer, although to that day she had never owned a camera. She had no idea where that idea came from ("My mind made itself up"), but the decision stuck. At her family's insistence, she entered a teacher's training program, although it held no interest for her; but soon after, she began to work in a photographer's studio and dropped out of the teaching program. In the next few years, she learned everything she could about photography, especially portraiture, by working in several studios, filling in on occasion as a photographer, and attending a class on photography taught by Clarence H. White. Nonetheless, she described herself as essentially self-taught. As she said in another context, although this "may sound like an immensely egotistical thing to say, I'm not aware photographically of having been influenced by anyone." [10]

In 1918, with her friend Florence Ahlstrom, she left New Jersey to work her way around the world as a photographer, possessing little more than determination to make such a plan feasible. For the first leg of their journey they traveled to New Orleans, and from there to San Francisco, where they promptly had all their money stolen. On their second day in San Francisco, Dorothea found a job in a photography shop, where she soon met Roi Partridge and his wife, Imogen Cunningham, who became her lifelong friends. Soon after, an investor named Sidney Franklin offered to back her in setting up her own portrait studio; she accepted. [11] Her business was almost immediately successful, and she began to photograph some of the wealthiest, most prominent families in San Francisco. At this time, too, when she was establishing herself as a photographer, she gave up her father's name, Nutzhorn, and took her mother's maiden name, Lange. Also in this period she was introduced by Roi Partridge to his friend, the Western painter Maynard Dixon, twenty-one years her senior. They were married in 1920; the marriage lasted fifteen years and produced two sons, Daniel and John.

During their marriage, Dixon was often away for extended periods on sketching and painting trips, sometimes taking Lange and the family with him, but more often not. Lange continued to photograph, maintaining her own studio for part of this time and keeping an active clientele. As she recalled, "[I] continued to reserve a small portion of my life . . . and that was my photographic area. Still, the most of life and the biggest part, the largest part of my energy, and my deepest allegiances, were to Maynard's work and my children." When the Depression began in the 1930s and their income dropped sharply, Dixon and Lange made the difficult decision to move into their respective studios and, more significantly, to put their young boys (ages four and seven) into a boarding school. This was "very, very hard for me to do. Even now [thirty years later] when I speak of it I can feel the pain. I carry these things inside, and it hurts me in the same spot that it did then." [12]

In 1932, with labor demonstrations taking place in San Francisco and breadlines forming nearly on her own doorstep, Lange ventured out on the street with her camera and began taking pictures. "They were made when I was just gathering my forces and that took a little bit because I wasn't accustomed to jostling about in groups of tormented, depressed and angry men, with a camera. Now I could do it much more easily because I've learned a lot about doing it, and I've confidence in people that they will trust me."[13] One of the pictures she took her first day out, "White Angel Breadline," remains one of the most powerful in her career [6.13]. Between 1932 and 1935, Lange's street photography was featured in two local exhibits, one in Oakland and the other in San Francisco. At the first of these, Paul Taylor saw her work and asked to include one of her photographs in an article he was writing on the San Francisco general strike. Lange readily agreed.

In 1935, she extended her collaboration with Paul Taylor, who was an economist at the University of California, Berkeley, by joining his staff on the State Emergency Relief Administration. Taylor, a forceful advocate for establishing camps for migrant workers, hired Lange to photograph farm laborers throughout the state of California. A report Taylor published on the plight of migrant workers, illustrated by Lange's photographs, came to the attention of Roy Stryker of the Farm Security Administration (FSA), who in turn invited Lange to become a staff photographer for the historical division of the newly formed administration. The FSA, like its predecessor, the Resettlement Administration, was an arm of the Department of Agriculture focusing on issues of rural poverty. Paul Taylor was appointed an advisor, and the collaboration between Taylor and Lange intensified. So, too, did their personal relationship. In 1935, Lange and Maynard Dixon were divorced, as were Paul Taylor and his wife, and Taylor and Lange married while on assignment in New Mexico.

Marriage to a university professor theoretically offered Lange the opportunity to settle into a domestic life—indeed, the combination of Taylor's three children and her own two might have dictated such a move—but, instead, Dorothea Lange embarked upon the most intense and productive phase of her career. Taylor and Lange continued the practice of boarding the children elsewhere, paradoxically, Taylor later reported, because "we wanted to establish as firm a *family* foundation as we could. Weekends, you see, we would have the children come to our home at 2706 Virginia Street."[14]

Much has been written about the Farm Security Administration and about Lange's contributions to the large archive of photographs recording the transformation of American agriculture and the western migration of sharecroppers, tenant farmers, and small-farm owners who were forced off their land by drought and mechanization. From the point of view of the photographers, the fledgling agency offered not only unprecedented opportunities but also tremendous freedom, which Lange found very appealing.

> *I found a little office, tucked away, in a hot, muggy, early summer, where nobody especially knew exactly what he was going to do or how he was going to do it. And this is no criticism, because you walked into an atmosphere of a very special kind of freedom; anyone who tells you anything else and dresses us up in official light is not truthful, because it wasn't that way. That freedom that there was, where you found your own way, without criticism from anyone, was special. That was germane to that project. That's the thing that is almost impossible to duplicate or find.*[15]

Working for the FSA also was fraught with difficulties and frustrations. Lange's long-distance relationship with Stryker required of her considerable diplomacy and tact.

An extensive correspondence between Roy Stryker and Dorothea Lange reveals that while they were always polite and cordial with one another, tensions and potentially explosive conflicts often smoldered just below the surface.

When Lange went into the field on assignment, she often had particular destinations in mind, or like the migrants themselves, she followed the harvest seasons through central California and up into Washington and Oregon. Once she was in the presence of the people she wanted to photograph, she talked to them about their circumstances, told them she was from the government, and asked their permission to take the pictures, usually a series of pictures. According to Ron Partridge, who sometimes accompanied her on field trips, the two of them would talk to people, Lange would take pictures, and then they would go off somewhere together and write down everything they could remember from the conversations, which in Lange's case resulted in extensive verbatim quotation. Based on these notes, Lange would later carefully write captions for all her photographs. Often the simple words of the people combined with the power of her visual images to form an eloquent and unprecedented collaboration between photographer and subject. Lange worked tirelessly during this period, traveling up and down the state of California, to Washington, D.C., to the South—Arkansas, Mississippi, and Alabama—and to the Dust Bowl—Arizona, New Mexico, Texas, and Oklahoma. Everywhere she went, she was constantly taking pictures, talking to displaced farm families, living a hard, exhausting life that she thrived on.

Dorothea Lange had a finely honed instinct that took her to the right place at the right time. The circumstances that brought her to make her most famous photograph, "Migrant Mother," illustrate the role that chance played in her career, and the ways she seized the opportunities that presented themselves to her.

> *It was raining, the camera bags were packed, and I had on the seat beside me in the car the results of my long trip, the box containing all those rolls and packs of exposed film ready to mail back to Washington. It was a time of relief. Sixty-five miles an hour for seven hours would get me home to my family that night, and my eyes were glued to the wet and gleaming highway that stretched out ahead. I felt freed, for I could lift my mind off my job and think of home.*
>
> *I was on my way and barely saw a crude sign with pointing arrow which flashed by at the side of the road, saying* PEA-PICKERS CAMP. *But out of the corner of my eye I did see it.*
>
> *I didn't want to stop, and didn't. I didn't want to remember that I had seen it, so I drove on and ignored the summons. Then, accompanied by the rhythmic hum of the windshield wipers, arose an inner argument:*
>
> Dorothea, how about that camp back there? What is the situation back there?
>
> Are you going back?
>
> Nobody could ask this of you, now could they?
>
> To turn back certainly is not necessary. Haven't you plenty of negatives already on this subject? Isn't this just one more of the same? Besides, if you take

a camera out in this rain, you're just asking for trouble. Now be reasonable, etc., etc., etc.

Having well convinced myself for 20 miles that I could continue on, I did the opposite. Almost without realizing what I was doing I made a U-turn on the empty highway. I went back those 20 miles and turned off the highway at that sign, PEA-PICKERS CAMP.

I was following instinct, not reason; I drove into that wet and soggy camp and parked my car like a homing pigeon.

I saw and approached the hungry and desperate mother, as if drawn by a magnet. I do not remember how I explained my presence or my camera to her, but I do remember she asked me no questions. I made five exposures, working closer and closer from the same direction. I did not ask her name or her history. She told me her age, that she was 32. She said that they had been living on frozen vegetables from the surrounding fields, and birds that the children killed. She had just sold the tires from her car to buy food. There she sat in that lean-to tent with her children huddled around her, and seemed to know that my pictures might help her, and so she helped me. There was a sort of equality about it.[16]

The photograph that ensued from this chance encounter was judged by Roy Stryker to be *the* photo of the FSA era.[17] It became the most famous photograph of the whole Depression era, and "perhaps the single most widely reproduced and popular photograph in our history"[18] [6.16].

The photograph enjoyed immediate success as well, but with a rather bizarre outcome. In September of 1936, her "Migrant Mother" was printed in *Survey Graphic* with Lange and the FSA receiving full credit for the work. But characteristic of her erratic relationship with Roy Stryker and the agency, and despite her obvious public success on behalf of the agency, the next month she was removed from the payroll. From this time until 1940, when the FSA dismissed her for the final time, her future within the agency was never secure. She was repeatedly dismissed, rehired, and dismissed again.

One FSA policy gave Lange particular trouble, namely, that the FSA held the rights to the work of its photographers; moreover, it held the negatives in its possession. The "Migrant Mother" photograph illustrates the frustrations this policy posed for Lange. She received repeated requests from publishers, museums, and curators to reprint the picture, and each time, she had to ask to borrow her own negative, to have it sent from Washington, D.C., to Berkeley so she could make her own prints. The first time she asked the agency to loan the negative to her she was told that the agency would make the print for her instead. This answer was clearly unacceptable: "This show is the most important photographic show we have. It tours the country. It tours Europe. I couldn't afford to show prints, unsigned, which I have never *seen*. I'll send the negative right back."[19] Her challenge here, as so many times later, was to walk the thinnest line because she was ultimately at the agency's mercy. She had to argue with sufficient force to convince the agency to reverse its decision about keeping the negative in its possession, yet she could not argue too forcefully or she would alienate those she had to persuade. She was always in danger of doing just that, but she sometimes prevailed.

The consequences of having limited access to her negatives went beyond issues of artistic control and an inverted power dynamic. At times it meant that she could not even see and assess her own work. When she was on assignment in the South, for example, she sent her exposed, undeveloped film directly to the FSA because the film deteriorated rapidly in the heat and humidity. As a result, she often had no idea how her work was turning out, or even whether her camera was working correctly in the same oppressive conditions that threatened the integrity of the film. Usually she received proof sheets of her work, but at other times she did not have even that. The most significant long-term consequence to her career was that her period of greatest productivity left her with almost nothing tangible in her possession: "I have nothing at all to show for my 3 years of government work in the way of prints," she wrote to Stryker.[20] As she continued in the same letter, her tone changed to resignation: "Wish I could have the time to make a few out of this new series for myself, but I expect you won't be able to permit it, or the time to do it, well, never mind." There were some battles she knew better than to pursue. The FSA, which has rightly been celebrated for the opportunity it provided to photographers such as Dorothea Lange, clearly required its people to pay a price.

In the last analysis, Lange's tug-of-war with Roy Stryker over her negatives and prints serves as a metaphor for the nature of their larger relationship; Lange, as artist and photographer, was always placed in a position of dependency on Stryker. It was altogether too easy for her to cross the thin line between requesting and insisting, yet her professional career demanded that she have greater access to and control over her own production. Her temperament would have led her to the same insistence—she was a powerful and forceful woman who knew her own mind. All things considered, it appears that she was a remarkably tactful woman in her dealings with Stryker.

More tangible obstacles faced Lange during this period, ranging from the difficulty of getting supplies to facing considerable personal danger on assignment. As she prepared to head down to the Imperial Valley in February of 1937 at the height of the migration of displaced workers into California, she wrote Stryker that "people continue to pour in and there is no way to stop them and no work when they get there." She told him that she planned to take a young assistant along with her. "Outsiders," she said, did not fare well there—some were given knockout drops, others were beaten up and left in ditches. "Down there it is too uncomfortable to be alone."[21] Having risked her safety to get negatives "loaded with ammunition," she learned that the FSA was reneging on the salary it had promised her. Sensitive to the inner workings of the bureaucracy but determined to speak out on her own behalf, she asked Stryker's permission to write to one of the agency's other chiefs to remind him of his promise to pay her $2,600. "I don't want to make difficult matters more difficult for you—Still I consider this rather shabby business, and I protest all this sort of treatment." Stryker's reply was telling. He acknowledged that she had indeed been offered $2,600 for her current assignment, but his indignation rang false: "It makes me sore as hell that I am put in a position of having to back down on a promise." But back down he did.[22]

In spite of her frustrations with the FSA, she exhibited a fine sense of humor, a playfulness and wit that allowed her to remain "properly" subordinate and maintain her sense of integrity. When threatened at one point with dismissal for apparent insubordination, she addressed her next letter to Stryker "Dear Boss." In another period, when she was not being paid for all the work she was doing, she signed herself "Your faithful slave."

Miffed that Stryker had never accompanied her on any of her field trips, as he had all the other photographers, she wrote to him from Texas, "You went with Rothstein, you went with Lee, you went with McAdams. And how about me?" In November of 1938 she again felt neglected by Stryker and complained, "This is the isolation ward as far as you are concerned." When an urgent request for darkroom equipment was apparently ignored in Washington, she realized that the only alternative left was to pay for her materials herself: "So saying, she pulled in her belt a couple of notches and said Good night."[23]

After five years of association with the FSA, she was let go for good by Stryker. In spite of an impassioned plea by two California agents on her behalf, citing among other things how much the agency owed to Paul Taylor, who was "still violently in love with Dorothea Lange," Stryker fired her. "I had to get rid of one photographer and I got rid of the least cooperative one." We have no record of Lange's personal response to this final turn of events, but in a letter to Stryker the following spring, she took the occasion to tell him how much she missed the FSA: "Once an FSA guy, always an FSA guy. You don't easily get over it."[24]

Lange's work for the FSA had totally engaged her. She brought a profound sense of social justice to her work, and as many passages in her letters to Stryker bear witness, she cared passionately (and eloquently) about the people she photographed. After repeated trips into the fields and camps and into the areas of the South and West from which so many people fled in desperation, she never seemed to be dulled by the human misery she witnessed. As critics over the years have noted of her work, she depicted not so much the misery or desperation of her subjects as their dignity and pride. Strangers were surprisingly at ease in her presence, and they trusted her.

Her choice to use primarily a Rolleiflex camera in the field contributed, too, to her ability to represent her subjects as fully realized human beings, but ones pushed to the edge. Held at her waist, not at eye level as a 35 mm camera would be, her Rolleiflex gave her an angle of vision that literally "looked up" at the people she photographed [6.29]. The angle enhanced the expanse of sky against which so many of her subjects are depicted, and it contributed to the sense of the heroic stature of her subjects, even in the face of incredible adversity. As she photographed people, she stood before them in a position of humility—her head bowed, with no intrusive gaze focused upon them. The interaction was quiet and respectful, and the results, for all of posterity, were photographs filled with compassion.

Disappointed by her dismissal from FSA but undaunted, Lange began to seek other outlets for her creative vision and her social concern. She conceived the notion of doing a series on select rural communities, including the Amana colonies in Iowa and the Mormons in Utah, and she applied for, and received, a Guggenheim Fellowship to support the project—the first woman photographer so honored [2.1, 2.2]. The greatest gift the fellowship offered her was a year in which to work "as a wholly free individual."[25] Unfortunately, after only two months and a photographic trip to the Amana colonies, she had to put her fellowship abruptly on hold in order to come to the aid of her brother, who had been arrested for his involvement with an unemployment insurance scam. Although the dream of completing the fellowship year lay before her for some time to come, she was never able to have that year of freedom.

In January of 1939, Lange saw her first major book project brought to fruition with the publication of *An American Exodus: A Record of Human Erosion.* This pioneering work

Mormon mother
who says she's
"been looking up at that old black ridge"
since 1877.
She has borne ten children.
Sitting with her husband on the steps of their old stone house
at evening,
she turned to him
and
quietly said,
"And none died, is there, Dad?"
And he,
as quietly,
answered,
"Yes, Jim died."

2.1.   Mormon Mother, 1953, by Dorothea Lange. Print courtesy Dorothea Lange Collection, The Oakland Museum, Oakland, California.

This is the road
that
runs through
her far-west village.

GUNLOCK, WASHINGTON COUNTY, UTAH. 1953

2.2.   Mormon Mother's Road, 1953, by Dorothea Lange. Print courtesy Dorothea Lange Collection, The Oakland Museum, Oakland, California.

represents an unparalleled collaboration between a photographer and a social scientist, between Dorothea Lange and Paul Taylor, and between the two of them and their photographic subjects. Taylor wrote the text of the book, Lange did the photography, and the persons photographed "spoke" through direct quotations. As Taylor and Lange wrote in their preface, "Our work is a product of cooperation in every aspect from the form of the whole to the last detail of arrangement or phrase."[26] The book includes some of the most enduring images from Lange's 1930s photography and, in effect, sums up a decade of American history, but its chance for any popular success was cut off by the fact that its publication coincided with the outbreak of World War II.

Lange's next year and a half as a photographer was spent in an unexpected and deeply troubling way. When President Franklin D. Roosevelt signed into law Executive Order 9066, the War Relocation Authority (WRA) rather inexplicably decided to document the registration, assembling, and internment of Japanese Americans. Ironically, Lange, whose most earnest hope had been to have a year of freedom for herself as a photographer, found herself working again for the government, photographing the "relocation" of Japanese Americans to internment camps. Along with Paul Taylor, she was outspoken in her opposition to the relocation, but the WRA hired her anyway.[27] Lange's record of the registration of Japanese Americans bears witness to her own sense of indignation and compassion, but more important, it captures the fierce pride and dignity of her subjects. It is as though all her experience photographing people in extreme distress was honed for this assignment. Her eye for the bitter ironies, for the telling details, was never finer; her sense of respect for her subjects never greater; her angle of vision never more appropriate [6.26–6.29].

Lange found the assignment "very, very difficult." It was filled with stories of personal tragedy. One story in particular stood out in her mind. A young man named Dave Tatsumo, a former University of California, Berkeley, student, allowed Lange to spend time with him and his family as they tried to put their affairs in order before reporting to the assembly center for removal to the camp at Topaz, Utah [2.3].

> *During this period, I was out on the street with him. He was taking me somewhere, and we met an old high school teacher of his. He greeted her and they stood and spoke, and I remember seeing a look go over her face and she said, 'Oh, but not you, Dave, they didn't mean you, Dave.' She didn't realize that he was going, too. To that degree, people lost their heads completely. I think of that 'Not you, Dave' many times."[28]*

After she photographed Bay Area Japanese Americans trying to sell their businesses, packing their personal belongings, registering with the government, and reporting to the assembly centers, Lange made three trips to the camp at Manzanar, California, in the first months of the camp's opening. She took volumes of photographs in all, several of them among the most poignant in her career. Even though she was working for the government, she was never allowed to be alone in the camps and was always accompanied by army guards. A government censor impounded some of her photographs, especially but not exclusively any that showed soldiers with guns or otherwise visually reinforced the fact that the Japanese Americans were really prisoners. Compared with many other

2.3. Dave Tatsumo, 1942, by Dorothea Lange. Print courtesy Bancroft Library, University of California, Berkeley.

photographs taken at Manzanar over the years, Lange's stand out as particularly honest and compassionate. She had no patience with the attitude toward the internment adopted by some of her colleagues, especially Ansel Adams. He never "got it," Lange declared—never understood what was wrong with the internment.[29]

When Lange finished her work for the WRA, she became a wartime photographer for a third government agency, the Office of War Information. Between 1943 and 1945 she was assigned to photograph a variety of ethnic communities in the United States. Unfortunately, the government lost most of the negatives from this project, so almost no record exists of this work. Other work she did in this period, however, has survived, and captures another aspect of the war effort closer to home, namely, shipbuilding and the way that enterprise transformed the town of Richmond, California. She conceived of the idea with Ansel Adams, and together the two of them undertook the assignment for *Fortune* magazine.

After that assignment, Dorothea's work came to a virtual standstill. For the next five years she was ill, at times desperately ill, with stomach ulcers. She was repeatedly hospitalized, and at least once hemorrhaged so severely she nearly died. She finally underwent surgery to remove the major portion of her stomach, an operation that no doubt saved her but that had long-term health implications. Symptoms of her illness had begun five years earlier; for long periods she was tired and in pain, but she was also driven. Without her terrific will, she might not have survived her illness, and certainly she would not have remained so active as a photographer.

After the war ended, and after recovering from her illness and surgery, Lange began to seek new directions for her photography. Certainly there was no question of laying her work aside; instead, she looked for new opportunities, for new subjects, and for new arenas for her talent. Because of her health limitations, she was forced to look closer to home for much of the time, but she remained fervently ambitious and adventuresome. She resumed photography in 1951, but it wasn't until 1953 that she was well enough to travel on assignment for *Life* magazine, this time to Utah, again with Ansel Adams [6.32, 6.33]. Her son Daniel Dixon assisted her on the trip, which led to the two of them next taking on an extended photographic assignment in Ireland, her first project outside the United States [6.34–6.37].

In 1954 she began another series for *Life,* this time featuring Martin Pulich, a lawyer in the Alameda County public defender's office. According to one account, her interest in how poor people were defended in the court system grew out of her experience with her brother's arrest and trial. As she became more familiar with the workings of the law, she began to consider the plight of those who could not afford to hire their own defense.[30] Martin Pulich was a wonderful photographic choice, as it turned out; he was a very serious and conscientious attorney, a warm and appealing young man. He let Lange follow him wherever his job took him; she received permission to photograph in the courtroom during trials, and even in the county jail. Characteristic of Lange's best work, the strength of these photos resides not in any sense of sensationalism or the drama of a murder trial, but in the intense and earnest face of Martin Pulich as he listened to his clients or as he sat lost in his own thoughts [2.4].

At about this time, she began a further project for *Life* that she ultimately entitled "The Death of a Valley." Because a major water supply was needed for the thousands of new residents who had settled in northern California during and following the war, in

2.4.   The Public Defender, Alameda County Courthouse, 1954, by Dorothea Lange.
Print courtesy Dorothea Lange Collection, The Oakland Museum, Oakland,
California.

1957 the government began to build a dam at the end of the Berryessa Valley, a rich farm valley northeast of San Francisco. The farms and communities of the valley were sacrificed to this end [2.5]. Lange and another photographer, Pirkle Jones, were on hand to record the last days of the valley—the farm auctions, the bulldozing of ancient valley oak trees, and ultimately the rising of the waters across once fertile farmlands. Although *Life* never ran the series, cutting it at the last moment to feature a flood in the South, the series was reproduced in a special issue of *Aperture,* a journal that Lange had helped found in 1952.[31] Work on the project was at times exhausting, and Lange's health was poor. She drove herself to the point of near collapse, but the result was a photoessay of the first order. It documented the human and ecological cost of "progress." Two of the most dramatic photos in the collection feature an old cemetery in the valley. The first photo shows wildflowers and grass growing up around the old gravestones; in its sequel, the graves lay open and raw after the bodies have all been removed to make way for the waters that would soon flood the valley [2.6, 2.7].

In the late 1950s and early 1960s, Paul Taylor's work took him to a number of developing countries. Although he went on some of the trips alone, he was particularly eager for Lange to join him on a six-month trip to Asia. Reluctantly, she agreed to go, although her health was very precarious and gave her considerable trouble on the trip. Later she would accompany Taylor on other trips—to Ecuador, to Egypt, to the Near East—always with some mixture of excitement and reluctance, and always eager to be home. Lange attempted to do work of her own, to photograph common human elements across cultures, but she met with countless frustrations. Nevertheless, she persisted. From Korea she wrote:

> *The #1 difficulty for me is that it is almost impossible for me to find ways to photograph on my own. This is not a country where one can circulate freely. Transportation is hard to get. Public transportation I cannot use. The buses (which are painted bright colors with big Korean designs on them—look like fierce dragons) are jammed with sweating humanity. There are no street names. I can't read the signs. Taxis, they tell me, are dangerous. You can't tell where you may land, and they are filthy, even if you can find one. The heat is a burden. I can have a government car* after hours, *but haven't found a way to work so that it fits in with all the other details one has to conform to as the wife of an official in a strange land.*[32]

The subjects in the best of her photographs from these trips abroad are curiously fragmented—a single hand gesturing, bare feet on a dusty road, a photograph of a child's face cropped so the top of his head is cut off. Perhaps the fragmentation reflects her unfamiliarity with the cultures she was photographing, perhaps her sense of her own body betraying her, but clearly it marks a transition in her photographic style as well as a new subject matter.

Dorothea Lange had recurring attacks of ulcers, and to add to the assault upon her body, while in the Near East she contracted malaria and had to be flown to Switzerland to be hospitalized. While her letters are full of brave cheer, it was clear that the greatest moment for her would be the return home to her family and her own world.

2.5. Woman from Berryessa Valley, California, Memorial Day, 1956, by Dorothea Lange. Print courtesy Dorothea Lange Collection, The Oakland Museum, Oakland, California.

2.6.   Cemetery, Berryessa Valley, California, 1956, by Dorothea Lange. Print courtesy
Dorothea Lange Collection, The Oakland Museum, Oakland, California.

GRAVEDIGGERS CAME INTO THE VALLEY.
THEY DISINTERRED BODIES FROM THE FAMILY PLOTS
AND CARRIED THEM DOWN THE ROAD, GRAVESTONES AND ALL,
TOWARD NEW PLOTS THAT HAD BEEN PREPARED ON HIGHER GROUND.   148

THE BIG OAKS WERE CUT DOWN
CATTLE HAD RESTED IN THEIR SHADE FOR GENERATIONS.
ON OLD MAPS AND DEEDS THEY HAD SERVED AS LANDMARKS.

2.7.   Open Graves, Berryessa Valley, California, 1956, by Dorothea Lange. Print courtesy Dorothea Lange Collection, The Oakland Museum, Oakland, California.

We are trying to get visas so that we can leave Asia about Jan. 1 by way of Moscow, Karachi, Kabul, Tashkent, Moscow, Berlin, London, New York, Washington, San Francisco, 1163 and HOME *by February 1st. It's getting closer and we're looking forward to it with joy. I'll be content to be there with my darlings forever. Paul not for forever but for a good long while and we have all this which we have experienced to think about and to re-live, for the rest of our lives.[33] [6.38–6.48].*

Now nearly sixty-five years old and in declining health, Dorothea Lange turned more to her family, especially the new generation of grandchildren, who became her final favorite photographic subjects. Her world was the world of her own backyard and her cabin at Steep Ravine at Stinson Beach [6.52, 6.53]. She envisioned producing a book of private family photographs, something like a photo album, as a tribute to and gift for her own family. But she was never to see the project through to completion; it was published (posthumously) as *To a Cabin* by her friend Margaretta Mitchell.[34] In keeping with her interest and her subjects, the photographs capture remarkably intimate moments and gestures. Over them there is a distinct sense of calm and contentment, of peace and, above all, a strong connection to her grandchildren that she never fully enjoyed with her own children.

In August of 1964 she was diagnosed with inoperable cancer of the esophagus. In the limited time left to her she took on two major projects. The first of these was the completion of *Dorothea Lange Looks at the American Country Woman,* a collection of photographs she had taken over the course of many years.[35] Published posthumously in 1967, the book presents a series of particularly striking portraits of country women, each photograph paired with another that depicts the subject's home or, if not the house itself, the landscape that represents her. The series is remarkable in its concept and execution. Lange understood how much of a woman's being was expressed in her domestic space, by the house in which she lived. She undertook this project even as she herself understood that the path she walked as a woman was completely different. She demonstrates in *The American Country Woman* her strong respect for and affinity with traditional women living out traditional women's roles.

Her most ambitious undertaking in this final year was preparing a retrospective of her work for the Museum of Modern Art. This work, while extremely demanding, was also fully engaging, and she was aided by several colleagues and family members. She wanted to lay the show out in groupings of photographs arranged not by chronology or even by obvious subject matter but by themes of her own devising. For once in her career, she had ready access to most, if not all, of her FSA negatives, and she had her own extensive files to sort through. Deciding what photographs to include and in what arrangement required an ongoing series of personal decisions and negotiations with the museum's photographic curator, John Szarkowski, who worked closely with her over a number of months. While their discussions were taking place, she also engaged in a series of interviews and filming sessions for the San Francisco station KQED, which produced two documentary films on her life and work. Even though in frequent and intense pain, and often too weak to continue without needing to lie down and rest, she worked at this project with much of the same drive and determination that had taken her through her full career. At the time of her death, most of the photos had been chosen and the prints had been made, much to her satisfaction. The retrospective opened in 1966 to wide acclaim.

In thinking back over her life, Dorothea Lange concluded her oral history by talking about her career as a woman photographer and by expressing regret that she had never had truly uninterrupted time in her career.

> *And I'm not focusing this entirely on myself, I'm speaking of the difference between the role of the woman as artist and the man. There is a sharp difference, a gulf. The woman's position is immeasurably more complicated. There are not very many first class women producers, not many. That is producers of outside things, they produce in other ways. Where they can do both, it's a conflict. I would like to try. I would like to have one year. I'd like to take one year, almost ask it of myself, 'Couldn't I have one year?' Just one, when I would not have to take into account anything but my own inner demands. Maybe everybody would like that . . . but I can't.*[36]

Dorothea Lange died on October 11, 1965, at the age of seventy.

NOTES

1. Interview of Lange by Richard K. Doud, May 22, 1964, transcript in Archives of American Art, Smithsonian Institution. Reprinted in *Dorothea Lange: Farm Security Administration Photographs, 1935–1939,* ed. Howard M. Levin and Katherine Northrup (Glencoe, Ill.: Text-Fiche Press, 1980), vol. 1, p. 85.

2. Interview of Rondal Partridge and Christina Gardner by Therese Heyman, August 1975, transcript in Dorothea Lange Collection, Oakland Museum, Oakland, Calif., vol. 2, pp. 61, 73.

3. Lange-Doud interview, p. 77.

4. Emphasis added. Lange to Roy Stryker, January 18, 1939, Dorothea Lange and Roy Stryker Correspondence, 1935–1944, Dorothea Lange Collection.

5. Interview of Ansel Adams by Therese Heyman, September 1976, transcript in Dorothea Lange Collection, vol. 1, p. 7.

6. Outtakes from the interviews of Dorothea Lange, 1963–1965, held in her home at 1163 Euclid Avenue, Berkeley, Calif., for two films produced for National Educational Television by KQED, Inc., San Francisco (*Closer for Me* and *Under the Trees*), tape 12, pp. 3–4. Copyright and all other rights held by Dorothea Lange Collection, The Oakland Museum, gift courtesy of Robert Katz and Paul Schuster Taylor.

7. Handwritten note by Dorothea Lange, n.d., in the possession of John Dixon.

8. Dorothea Lange, *The Making of a Documentary Photographer,* an oral history interview conducted in 1960 and 1961 by Suzanne Riess (Berkeley: Regional Oral History Office, Bancroft Library, University of California, Berkeley, 1968), p. 177.

9. Lange, *Making of a Documentary Photographer,* pp. 6–7.

10. Lange-Doud interview, p. 58.

11. Milton Meltzer, *Dorothea Lange: A Photographer's Life* (New York: Farrar, Straus & Giroux, 1978), p. 46.

12. Lange, *Making of a Documentary Photographer,* pp. 97, 141.

13. Ibid., p. 149.

14. Emphasis added. Interview of Paul Taylor by Suzanne Riess, 1973, transcript in Regional Oral History Office, Bancroft Library, University of California, Berkeley, p. 150.

15. Lange-Doud interview, p. 64.

16. Dorothea Lange, "The Assignment I'll Never Forget: Migrant Mother," *Popular Photography* 46, no. 2 (February 1960), pp. 42–43, 128. Quoted in Meltzer, *Dorothea Lange,* pp. 131–32.

17. Meltzer, *Dorothea Lange,* p. 133.

18. Lawrence W. Levine, "The Folklore of Industrial Society: Popular Culture and Its Audiences," *American Historical Review* 97, no. 5 (December 1992), p. 1386.

19. Lange to Stryker, September 10, 1936, Dorothea Lange and Roy Stryker Correspondence, 1935–1944, Dorothea Lange Collection.

20. Lange to Stryker, October 20, 1937, ibid.

21. Lange to Stryker, February 16, 1937, ibid.

22. Lange to Stryker, March 17, 1937, ibid.

23. Lange to Stryker, November 19, 1936; April 14, 1937; June 9, 1937; November 5, 1938; November 6, 1938, ibid.

24. Jonathan Garst to Stryker, November 21, 1939; Stryker to Garst, November 30, 1939; Lange to Stryker, March 31, 1940, ibid.

25. Guggenheim Fellowship Application, Dorothea Lange Collection.

26. Dorothea Lange and Paul S. Taylor, *An American Exodus: A Record of Human Erosion in the Thirties* (New Haven: Yale University Press, published for the Oakland Museum, 1969), p. 15.

27. Christina Gardner later observed, "Paul and Dorothea were the only people that I heard of in the USA that stood up publicly and made waves about the Japanese evacuation." Partridge-Gardner-Heyman interview, p. 60.

28. Lange, *Making of a Documentary Photographer,* pp. 193–94. Lange reported in the interview that Dave Tatsumo lost a child because of exposure in the Topaz camp and that "his life is dedicated to the memory of that child."

29. Lange's and Adams's Manzanar photographs make an interesting study of contrasts. See, for example, Karin Becker Ohrn, *Dorothea Lange and the Documentary Tradition* (Baton Rouge: Louisiana State University Press, 1980), pp. 122–46.

30. Meltzer, *Dorothea Lange,* p. 298.

31. Dorothea Lange and Pirkle Jones, "Death of a Valley," *Aperture* 8 (1960), pp. 127–65.

32. Lange to Helen Dixon, August 6, 1958, Lange Family Letters, June 1958–February 1959, Dorothea Lange Collection.

33. Lange to Helen and John Dixon, November 29, 1958, ibid.

34. Dorothea Lange and Margaretta K. Mitchell, *To a Cabin* (New York: Grossman, 1973).

35. *Dorothea Lange Looks at the American Country Woman* (Fort Worth: Amon Carter Museum; Los Angeles: The Ward Ritchie Press, 1967).

36. Lange, *Making of a Documentary Photographer,* p. 220.

Clark Kerr

PAUL AND DOROTHEA

Dorothea, a few weeks before her death, came to our house on a Sunday afternoon. She said she would like to make prints of her photographs—two per person—and then frame them, as gifts for a few close friends. She was very businesslike. My wife chose pictures of members of the joint families of Paul and Dorothea. I chose two, each of which reflected my connections with Paul and through Paul with Dorothea. One was "White Angel Breadline" [6.13], for Paul and I had studied together the unemployed in the Great Depression, particularly their self-help cooperatives in California. It was through these studies that Paul first worked with Dorothea. The second was "Migrant Mother" [6.16], for Paul and I had also worked together studying migratory farm workers. These two photos have been, side by side, on my office wall for many years now.

I knew Paul S. Taylor and Dorothea Lange for all of the thirty years of their life together, and saw Paul's influence on Dorothea and Dorothea's on Paul. Their work together is a part of American history, as they recorded American history in the making.

Paul was an explorer, not of seas and islands and continents, but of, up until then, almost unnoticed social events as they began to take form. He was the first, or among the first, to put several of these events on the map of history, to make them part of terra cognito. He began with the early migration of Mexicans to California, to south Texas, to Colorado, to Chicago, to Bethlehem, Pennsylvania, in a series of studies published by the University of California (1928–1932). Then he went to Mexico to see points of origins of this migration. The trickle of that time has become a torrent, and by the end of the first decade of the next century, the schools of California will be more Hispanic than Anglo [3.1, 3.2].

He turned then to the unemployed, when one-quarter of the American labor force was fully unemployed and another one-quarter was partially unemployed. At that time most economists had a model, and were teaching a model, of the economy (as I was being taught) that called for an automatic equilibrium at full employment! Paul was looking at reality while they were still looking at their model. He was later to quote Carleton Parker, his predecessor at Berkeley, as saying that "the sin of economics has been the divorce of its work from reality."[1]

It was at this point that I first met Paul. I was a graduate student in economics at Stanford (1932–1933), writing a master's thesis on the self-help cooperatives of the unemployed. Faculty members were friendly, but not one was interested professionally in the unemployed. I heard that there was a professor at Berkeley who was interested. I went to see him and he invited me to Berkeley to be his research assistant starting in the fall of 1933. He was particularly interested in a self-help cooperative in Oroville, California, called the Unemployed Exchange Association (UXA) [3.3]. He later invited Dorothea to visit UXA with him and record its existence with her photographs. She had already shown her interest in the unemployed with her photograph "White Angel Breadline."

3.1.   Paul Taylor Interviewing Migrant Family, early 1930s, by Dorothea Lange, printed by Ron Partridge from the original negative.

3.2.   Cotton Workers, location unknown, early 1920s, by Paul S. Taylor, printed by Ron Partridge from the original negative.

3.3.   Unemployed Exchange Association, Oroville, California, 1934, by Dorothea
Lange. Courtesy Dorothea Lange Collection, The Oakland Museum, Oakland,
California.

My next connection with Paul involved agricultural labor. I had hardly arrived in Berkeley in the fall of 1933 when the largest and bloodiest strike of agricultural workers in American history began in the San Joaquin Valley among cotton pickers [3.4]. I spent six weeks in the valley, and Paul came down on weekends. He gave me only two instructions: to record what people said—their own words—and to send him my notes as soon as possible. I gathered later that these were the same instructions Paul first gave to Dorothea, except that she worked with photographs and I with notes.

Paul and Dorothea later went on to explore the impact of the cotton picking machine and the boll weevil on what had been King Cotton in the South and on the people who had served King Cotton, and of the wind and the tractor on the Okies and Arkies and Texans and on the farm families of the Great Plains more generally, and of the development of the "factories in the fields" in California. Their book *An American Exodus: A Record of Human Erosion* (1939) was one result.[2] It chronicled, in words and photographs, a changing nation never again to be the same. They were there and they recorded it for all time just as it was. They went on to record the sadly relocated Japanese Americans in Manzanar during World War II and other groups of people and individuals caught in the pressures of great forces, both of natural and human origins beyond their control, and how they reacted.

Paul and Dorothea had complementary skills but contrasting personalities. She was always moving, mostly talking, reacting in a flash, living in the moment. Paul thought carefully about everything, spoke seldom and then softly. An illustration: During the cotton pickers' strike, I drove him back to Berkeley one Sunday night in my Model A Ford roadster. We stopped at a rural gas station, and he got out. Another identical car drove up and the male driver also got out. I was asleep in the front seat of my car and woke as the driver of the second car—now missing—yanked open the door, grabbed me by the throat, and wanted to know what I had done with his wife. Once I caught on to the situation, I wanted to know what he had done with my professor. Some time later, Paul drove up and got into my car, and off we went to Berkeley. I sat there wondering: Did the wife wake up screaming? Did he suddenly realize that his research assistant was not female? He never said a word all the way to Berkeley, as though nothing had happened worth noting.

This leads me to Paul's interests and methods, and the impact of both on Dorothea's interests and methods. Paul was listed as an economist at Berkeley—which, strictly defined, he was not. He was, rather, a social scientist trained at the University of Wisconsin during the "progressive era" of the La Follettes as an economist (under John R. Commons) and as a sociologist (under E. A. Ross) but with additional interests in law and public policy. He also had, as he said in his oral history, a "strong sense of history," which was also true of Commons.[3] He was really a historian of the contemporary, specializing in labor history with special attention to agriculture. He was, when I first met him, among the least noticed of professors in the social sciences at Berkeley; now he is among the most remembered in a broader world.

His interest was in change—in what was changing, in how history was being remade. His method consisted of taking snapshots and verbatim notes. He began taking photographs in Mexico with his old Rolleiflex. He carried it with him in the San Joaquin Valley when we were preparing our history of the cotton pickers' strike and used some of his photos as illustrations. This history is included in Taylor's book *On the Ground in*

3.4.   Loading Cotton, California, 1936, by Dorothea Lange. Library of Congress, LC USF34 9959.

the Thirties (1989), which includes another of our joint efforts, an article entitled "Uprisings on the Farms," illustrated with his photographs.[4] His passion was absolute accuracy—in his notes and my notes, in his photographs and, later, Dorothea's photographs. This meant no interviews with set questions in logical order but a friendly conversation that covered all the points, no posed photographs but snapshots of people in the ordinary conduct of their lives.

Paul first came in contact with the photographs of Dorothea in the summer of 1934. In the gallery of Willard Van Dyke in Oakland he saw a photograph of hers that he wanted for an article in *Survey Graphic* on the San Francisco general strike earlier that year. He met her and arranged for the photograph to be the frontispiece for the article. This led to his asking her to help record the work of the UXA self-help cooperative and subsequently the conditions surrounding the pea pickers' strike in San Luis Obispo County ("Migrant Mother" was taken in the strikers' camp). And there followed thirty years of collaboration around the nation and around the world.

The photograph by Dorothea that Paul first wanted was of a strike orator; the *Survey Graphic* editors gave the photograph the title "Workers Unite!" Dorothea was then an inside-the-studio portrait photographer of local fame in San Francisco, but as a side interest, she had started to go out into the streets in the deep Depression years. Thus she was already moving toward Paul's history-in-the-making interests before she met him. Their joint interests moved her all the way in that direction, and she became one of the great documentary photographers of all time.

Why had she started to move in that direction before she met Paul? Some said it was because of her left-wing intellectual convictions. I do not believe that at all; she was one of the most nonideological persons I have ever known. In thirty years, I never heard one word or saw one gesture that in any way indicated that she was a committed ideologue. Yet Ansel Adams, in his autobiography, wrote, "I recall many discussions among our close friends and colleagues as to whether she leaned to Leninism or Trotskyism and whether she was a Communist Party member or not." (Ansel Adams, it should be noted, admired her work and called her photographs "emotional documents.")[5] Dorothea says in her oral history that she was not a party member, partly because of the influence of her then husband, Maynard Dixon.[6] She says, however, that she had "many encounters" with Communists seeking her participation with them and that "I'm not sure it wasn't the right thing to do in those days."[7] Those were the days of mass unemployment in the United States and the rise of Hitler in Germany. Her excellent biographer, Milton Meltzer, writes, "Had she taken the step, it is unlikely that she would ever have submitted to party discipline for long."[8] I totally agree. She accepted discipline from no one but herself: "I have a great instinct for freedom."[9]

Paul Taylor is recorded as saying, in answer to the question "Was she interested in politics?," "The answer is no."[10] What she was interested in was people, and she was enormously empathetic with them, as her photographs show. And it would have taken a cold heart or a political orientation shorn of empathy or both not to be interested in the unemployed or in agricultural laborers at that time and place in history. Paul was an old-line Jeffersonian Democrat, committed to democracy based on the family farm and on a universal elementary education. So was I.

Paul did have political interests in addition to human compassion. As a Jeffersonian, he was appalled at mass unemployment and at exploitation in the fields and of the fields.

This was not the America he had fought for in World War I as a lieutenant in the marines, commanding a platoon with 95 percent casualties, himself one of them, at Chateau Thierry and Belleau Wood. (He prized his marine uniform all his life.) Paul was also the subject of red-baiting due to his support of sanitary labor camps for agricultural workers and his long opposition to the illegal diversion of water intended for family farms to the owners of the vast "factories in the fields." He was asked in his oral history whether he was suspected of being a Communist. He replied: "Why, of course! Of course . . . the FBI was being used to try to 'get' me."[11]

Paul was consequently astonished when I persuaded the Board of Regents of the University of California to grant him an honorary degree (1965) and then told him I had met some questioning but no organized opposition. My citation described him as "a labor economist, with special competence in problems of rural and migratory workers, and in the effects of changing technology on agricultural labor. His studies are marked by broad human sympathies, a wealth of practical observation and experience, and careful, objective analysis of detail."

The honorary degree was for Paul; the date was for Dorothea—June 15, 1965. She died early the next fall. Dorothea arranged a big family reunion (the last) for Paul after the commencement ceremonies, and she was very proud of Paul and joyful for him. My wife, Kay, and I were the two nonfamily members included. The citation was intended for, and described, both Paul and Dorothea: "broad human sympathies," "wealth of practical observation," "careful, objective analysis of detail."

Paul's original interest in Dorothea stemmed from his interest in the "camera as a tool of research."[12] It became far more than that. It became a great love affair. Paul, in retrospect, said: "It was always a wonderful thing to see her, always. Just to come into the room where she was."[13] Years later, I would visit Paul in the old redwood house on Euclid Avenue which Dorothea had chosen for them, and as Paul played Beethoven softly on his hi-fi set, we would talk about being "on the ground in the thirties." Dorothea's name would come up and Paul would sit there with tears streaming down his face as I recalled his tender words—"just to come into the room where she was."

Dorothea in her very last days said what a pleasure it was to take a picture and to see that what you have done "is true" and that she believed she could "see straight, and true, and fast."[14] Paul and Dorothea wrote, in *An American Exodus,* "We have let them speak to you face to face."[15] The "them" were the unemployed man in the breadline; the migrant mother and the children clinging to her; the Okie in the Model T Ford, moving west, fleeing the dust; the Mexicans living alongside the irrigation ditches; the Japanese Americans crowded into the detention camps. Through the notes and the photographs of Paul and Dorothea, we are indeed brought "face to face" with "them" and with their histories, which are a part of the history of our nation, and we know that what we read and see is true.

That is how I knew Paul and Dorothea.

1. Paul S. Taylor, in *There Was Light: Autobiography of a University, Berkeley: 1868–1968,* ed. Irving Stone (Garden City, N.Y.: Doubleday, 1970), p. 35.

2. Dorothea Lange and Paul S. Taylor, *An American Exodus: A Record of Human Erosion* (New York: Reynal and Hitchcock, 1939).

3. Paul Schuster Taylor, *California Social Scientist,* oral history interview conducted by Suzanne B. Riess and Malca Chall, 3 vols. (Berkeley: Regional Oral History Office, Bancroft Library, University of California, Berkeley, 1973 and 1975), vol. 1, p. 162.

4. Paul S. Taylor, *On the Ground in the Thirties* (Salt Lake City: Gibbs M. Smith, 1989). Also Paul S. Taylor and Clark Kerr, "Uprisings on the Farms," *Survey Graphic* 24 (January 1935), pp. 19–22.

5. Ansel Adams, with Mary Street Alinder, *Ansel Adams: An Autobiography* (Boston: Little, Brown, 1983), p. 266.

6. Dorothea Lange, *The Making of a Documentary Photographer,* an oral history interview conducted in 1960 and 1961 by Suzanne Riess (Berkeley: Regional Oral History Office, Bancroft Library, University of California, Berkeley, 1968), pp. 151–52.

7. Ibid.

8. Milton Meltzer, *Dorothea Lange: A Photographer's Life* (New York: Farrar, Straus & Giroux, 1978), p. 78.

9. Outtakes from the interviews of Dorothea Lange, 1963–1965, held in her home at 1163 Euclid Avenue, Berkeley, Calif., for two films produced for National Educational Television by KQED, Inc., San Francisco (*Closer for Me* and *Under the Trees*), tape 8, p. 160. Copyright and all other rights held by Dorothea Lange Collection, The Oakland Museum, gift courtesy of Robert Katz and Paul Schuster Taylor.

10. Taylor, *California Social Scientist,* p. 222.

11. Ibid., p. 304.

12. Lange and Taylor, *An American Exodus,* p. 6.

13. Taylor, *California Social Scientist,* pp. 226–27.

14. Lange, *Making of a Documentary Photographer,* pp. 217, 328.

15. Lange and Taylor, *An American Exodus,* p. 6.

4

Roger Daniels

DOROTHEA LANGE AND THE WAR RELOCATION AUTHORITY

Photographing Japanese Americans

What I photographed was the procedure, the process of processing. I photographed the normal life insofar as I could. . . . I photographed . . . the Japanese quarter of San Francisco, the businesses as they were operating, and the people as they were going to their YWCAs and YMCAs and churches and in their Nisei headquarters, all the baffled, bewildered people. . . . I photographed the long lines on the streets waiting . . . for the inoculations, down Post Street and around the corner. . . . I photographed when they all were gathered together at the assembly centers—the actual practical arrangements that had to be made. . . . I photographed them on the buses, on the trains and I photographed their arrival in the assembly centers. . . . I photographed only one of the interior centers, Manzanar, in Owens Valley.

—Dorothea Lange, 1968

I t is often forgotten that the War Relocation Authority (WRA), originated by President Franklin D. Roosevelt's executive order in March 1942 to oversee the incarceration of the West Coast Japanese Americans, was, in many respects, a typical New Deal "alphabet" agency.[1] It was created for a relatively short time for a specific purpose and was staffed by persons who were almost all without the kinds of permanent employment that much government work gives. Its leaders were, more or less, New Dealers who believed in the positive nature of the role of the federal government. One or two of them, such as its first director, Milton S. Eisenhower, at least had inklings that they might be involved in something awful. As he wrote privately to his former boss Claude Wickard, Roosevelt's second secretary of agriculture, as the roundup of Japanese Americans was beginning, "I feel most deeply that when the war is over and we consider calmly this unprecedented migration of 120,000 people, we as Americans are going to regret the unavoidable injustices that may have been done."[2]

But he never criticized the policy of incarceration publicly during the war. And even Eisenhower, surely one of the most thoughtful of the WRA administrators, had so deluded himself about what he had helped to establish that he was able to write in his memoirs, some thirty years later, that "we called the relocation camps 'evacuation centers.' Never did we think of them as concentration camps. Technically, the Japanese-Americans were not restricted to the camps, although in fact they could not return to the Pacific coast and movement without safeguards would probably have endangered their lives, at least at the beginning." [3]

Although it is clear that in 1942 most Americans approved what was being done to Japanese Americans—and would have approved worse—the verdict of history, and eventually of the American government itself, has been quite different. In 1982 a presidential commission, after a long investigation, issued the following verdict:

> [The incarceration of Japanese Americans] was not justified by military necessity, and [was] not driven by analysis of military conditions. The broad historical causes which shaped these decisions were race prejudice, war hysteria and a failure of political leadership. Widespread ignorance of Japanese Americans contributed to a policy conceived in haste and executed in an atmosphere of fear and anger at Japan. A grave injustice was done to Americans and resident aliens of Japanese ancestry who, without any individual review or probative evidence against them, were excluded, removed and detained by the United States during World War II. [4]

Acting on the presidential commission's report five years later, Congress passed and President Ronald W. Reagan signed a law which not only issued an apology but authorized a tax-free payment of twenty thousand dollars to each survivor of incarceration.

As was the case with most New Deal agencies, the WRA saw photography as a way of getting favorable images of its activities before the public. Milton Eisenhower had come to the WRA from the Department of Agriculture, which had long used both still and motion picture photography to promote its message, so it is not surprising that he soon arranged for a number of photographers to record the uprooting of the West Coast Japanese. Among those hired was Dorothea Lange. Although Lange apparently remained on the staff of the WRA for a year and a half—that would be until September 1943—she took the vast majority of her surviving images between March and September 1942. Most depict the Japanese American people on the eve of their incarceration and the process by which they were rounded up and shipped off to the holding pens called assembly centers [4.1].

Later Lange and the most celebrated photographer of the time, Ansel Adams, made a joint visit to the concentration camp at Manzanar, California. [5] Adams's insistence on publishing during the war the photographs he took there in a book called *Born Free and Equal* was an act of courage. However, unlike Lange, Adams was willing to make excuses for the government, insisting in 1944 that Manzanar was "only a rocky wartime *detour* on the road of American citizenship, . . . a symbol of the whole pattern of relocation—a vast expression of government working to find a suitable haven for its war-dislocated minorities." [6]

The photographic program of the WRA continued throughout its existence, and there are perhaps 12,500 prints now stored, arranged by subject and site, and accessible in the National Archives. [7] The overwhelming majority of these are routine public relations photographs, designed to document buildings, personnel, and certain ceremonial events. They emphasize the positive, what William Dean Howells once called "the smiling

4.1.   Some of the first group of Japanese Americans to be evacuated from San Fran-
cisco waiting at 2020 Van Ness Avenue for buses to take them to an assembly center,
April 6, 1942. The man on the right facing camera is Mike Masaoka, an official of the
Japanese American Citizens League. By Dorothea Lange. WRA photograph, Still
Picture Division, National Archives.

aspects of life."[8] If we judge from the images themselves, we must conclude that almost none of the photographers, some of whom were on the WRA payroll and some of whom were free-lancers hired for a specific assignment, seem to have had any notion that they were recording an American tragedy. One is reminded of Hannah Arendt's phrase about the banality of evil. People were photographed as if they were on an extended holiday or at a company picnic. Rarely were barbed wire, watchtowers, and armed soldiers depicted.[9] And, as Sylvia E. Danovitch, author of the best essay on WRA photographs, has pointed out, not one photograph exists among the many thousands in the National Archives, of the infamous assembly center toilets without partitions or individual privacy, which caused both psychological and physical distress among many of the women inmates. She did discover that Lange had photographed an outhouse at Manzanar but that the WRA had stamped that photo "impounded" so that it was never released.[10]

Among the thousands of WRA images that I have looked at, the work of two photographers, one famous and one unknown, stand in strong contradistinction to these generalizations. One, of course, is Dorothea Lange; the other is Clem Albers.[11] Just from looking at their images we understand not only that each disapproved of uprooting thousands of innocent men, women, and children, more than two-thirds of whom were native-born American citizens, but also that each knew that something awful was being perpetrated. How was it was that these two photographers—and a relatively few other Americans—were alive to this problem when such establishment figures as Eisenhower, as he later confessed, "spent little time pondering the moral implications" of incarcerating Japanese?

Obviously nothing can be said about the views of the still little-known Albers, but we know that Lange and her husband Paul Taylor not only opposed the removal and incarceration of Japanese Americans and spoke out against it, but also had Japanese American friends with whom they corresponded.[12] In the spring of 1942 Taylor, a professor at the University of California, Berkeley, joined in an unsuccessful remonstrance to President Roosevelt initiated by John Dewey and others of the Post War World Council, urging that all Japanese Americans, alien and citizen, be given "a hearing before civilian boards to attest their loyalty" before being ousted from their homes.[13] That fall Taylor published one of the first articles at all sympathetic to the Japanese American victims of the incarceration to appear in a nationally circulated magazine. Throughout the war he acted as an advocate for their better treatment and release, and later was an active member of the Fair Play Committee, which tried to make the painful return to California easier.[14] The returnees, who thanks to a belated Supreme Court decision were able to come back in January 1945, drew hostility from many if not most Californians. In an extreme example of verbal abuse the Auburn *Journal Republican* editorialized that "to say it is our duty to civilize, humanize and Christianize the Japs is just bunk. If we must do something for them, let us sterilize them." In addition, there was a lot of night-rider violence against returning Japanese, often led by rural law enforcement officers.[15]

Apart from the fact that Lange provided pictures for Taylor's 1942 article, I know of no surviving contemporary written evidence that she shared his views, which she assuredly did. "It was shameful," she told Suzanne Riess years later.[16] Lange wrote with her camera, not with her pen. But in addition to the testimony of her pictures, we have the evidence of Christina Gardner, who accompanied Lange on most of the shoots she made to photograph the Japanese Americans.[17]

Lange herself did not remember the precise circumstances of her hiring but did remember that she had worked "under Milton Eisenhower," who was in the Bay Area for several weeks of his brief WRA tenure.[18] As we have seen, he was attuned to photographic publicity, and he may well have known of or even known Lange, who had worked for his department's Farm Security Administration and its Bureau of Agricultural Economics. He himself appeared in a self-serving Office of War Information motion picture short subject made to explain the "relocation" to the public.

Christina Gardner remembers that after almost two months of shooting at various locations in northern and central California, Lange was nearly overwhelmed by the quiet horror of what she had been photographing. Gardner recalled that, in the Woodland Hotel in Woodland, Yolo County, on the evening of May 23, 1942,

> I took Paul [Taylor's] little old portable typewriter down to the lobby and when I went back up to the room, Dorothea was in some sort of paroxysm of fear. . . . She realized that this was such an erosion of civil liberties, she had gotten so consumed by it and realized the import of it so heartily that it was something that I cannot explain to this day. I've never seen her that way before or since, I never saw somebody that was in such a state.

By the morning, however, Lange had pulled herself together and went on to another day of shooting. As Gardner described it:

> The next day we went to the railroad station and as always all those Japanese people whose lives were being cut off—they were going to a concentration camp—think of how they felt. They didn't know how they were going to get treated. . . . They couldn't imagine what it was going to be like. . . . They were such good citizens. They patiently stood in line and the MPs . . . would do a little shoving when the crowds got heavy and it was touchy. . . . There were curious onlookers and you knew that there were people there who were glad to see them going. Especially in those country places. . . . The people often didn't understand what was being said to them. . . . They were getting on a train[19] which was a different departure from a lot of buses that we had seen in Oakland and other areas go to [the camp at] Tanforan.[20]

Perhaps because Lange's empathy with the Japanese American victims of the wartime incarceration was clear, she was viewed with suspicion by MPs, army officers, some WRA officials, and, ironically, by at least one evacuee. Charles Kikuchi, admittedly a very unusual Japanese American, made the following entry in his diary for April 30, 1942, while he and the last of the Berkeley Japanese Americans were waiting for a bus to take them to the assembly center at Tanforan: "Oh, oh, there goes a 'thing' in slacks and she is taking pictures of that old Issei lady with a baby. She says she is the official photographer, but I think she ought to leave these people alone."[21] On the other hand, according to Gardner: "The Japanese accepted her as one of them. . . . I never heard anybody object to being photographed by her. . . . She was a quiet woman and . . . she melted into

4.2.   Issei Mother. This Japan-born woman and her American-born children in Hayward, California, waiting for a bus to take them to an assembly center, May 8, 1942. By Dorothea Lange. WRA photograph, Still Picture Division, National Archives.

crowds. . . . She would take pains to explain 'I'm photographing for the United States government and they wish me to make a record of what is happening.'"[22]

In addition to Gardner's testimony we have a number of letters to Lange and sometimes to her and Paul Taylor from inmates of concentration camps and from resettled Japanese testifying to what is clearly mutual affection and regard. A group of letters from Masago Shibuya contains a poignant passage in a March 1943 letter from the camp at Heart Mountain, Wyoming. After telling "Mr. and Mrs. Taylor" about the death of her mother, Shibuya asks "a great favor":

> *The last photographs which were made of my mother were the series that you took just previous to our evacuation. Could it be possible for us to secure a set of the pictures. . . . Her passing was just one of those things that we never even dreamt of in our worst nightmares—we had just supposed that we should all be returning to California soon—but now even California has lost much of its allure—for California holds so much that is Mother.*[23]

We don't know if the pictures were ever sent or if the surviving Shibuyas ever returned to California, but we do know that both Paul and Dorothea filled out the recommendations (preferably from Caucasians) that were a necessary part of the process of resettlement and that the surviving Shibuyas were, by mid-1943, resettled in Colorado, Iowa, and Illinois. It is possible but not probable that the elder Shibuya is the central figure in the photograph I have had the temerity to title "Issei Mother" [4.2].

In any event, that picture, which I do not believe has been reproduced previously, is representative of one part of Lange's collective depiction of the Japanese American experience, a depiction which seems to have begun and ended with her WRA stint. She always strove to show Japanese Americans as persons of dignity who had achieved a modest competence by hard work. "Issei Mother," whoever she is, is shown head upraised, with her accomplishment—her adult and obviously middle-class children—in clear focus behind her. It is a portrait of a proud woman, and only Lange's caption informing us of the circumstances causes us to look again to see how this person faces adversity. Previous sequences of Lange's Japanese American pictures show us a community on the eve of its destruction—destruction not by the enemy but by its own government. These pictures are compelling, like those even more compelling pictures of the shtetls of eastern Europe in 1941, because we, the viewers, know what is about to happen. The last part of Lange's work shows the evacuation process—the notices, the lines, the soldiers, the piles of baggage, the trains, the buses, the trucks, and the deplorable quarters in which the Japanese American people were housed, like the horse stalls still stinking of manure at the Tanforan race track in which the United States Army forced some American families to live.[24]

These images of Lange's are quite different from those of Ansel Adams. In the first place, the entirety of Adams's Japanese American work is restricted to one time and place: the concentration camp at Manzanar, California, in the fall of 1943. In the second place, unlike Lange, who was from first to last primarily a photographer of persons, Adams was primarily a photographer of places. Even when his focus is a human being, the result is more like a portrait of a statue than a picture of a person. And because he was a superb photographer of the environment, his luminous landscapes make Manzanar seem more beautiful and interesting than it really was. Professional photographers and students of photography may conclude, as Danovitch does, that "the work of Dorothea Lange is no more or less effective than that of Ansel Adams although Lange was experienced at exposing social injustice with a camera. Lange's WRA work depends heavily upon the prose that accompanies it. Both Adams and Lange succeeded to the extent that they focused on the faces of the internees, dispelling their anonymity and allowing the viewer to identify with them as human beings." [25]

The social historian is not likely to share that view. We are fortunate to have the work of Adams and Lange (and the other largely unknown photographers of the wartime ordeal of the Japanese Americans, including that of the "illegal" inmate photographer of Manzanar, Toyo Miyatake). [26] But if we had to choose the work of just a single photographer to inform ourselves and posterity of what the wartime experience of the Japanese Americans was like, it would be that of Dorothea Lange. We can say this on the basis of her published work, even though only a minor fraction of her Japanese American corpus has ever been seen outside of the National Archives.

NOTES

1. The War Relocation Authority was created by Executive Order 9102, March 18, 1942. The initial executive order that led to the incarceration of the Japanese Americans was 9066, February 19, 1942. The most recent account of the ordeal of the Japanese American people is Roger Daniels, *Prisoners without Trial: Japanese Americans in World War II* (New York: Hill & Wang, 1993).

2. Milton S. Eisenhower to Claude Wickard, April 1, 1942, Correspondence of the Secretary of Agriculture, Foreign Relations, 2–2, Aliens-Refugees, Record Group 16, National Archives.

3. Milton S. Eisenhower, *The President Is Calling* (New York: Doubleday, 1974), p. 122. The best biography of Eisenhower is Stephen E. Ambrose and Richard H. Immerman, *Milton S. Eisenhower: Educational Statesman* (Baltimore: Johns Hopkins University Press, 1983).

4. Commission on Wartime Relocation and Internment of Civilians, *Personal Justice Denied* (Washington, D.C.: Government Printing Office, 1982).

5. Lange had been to the Manzanar camp perhaps twice before. Dorothea Lange, *The Making of a Documentary Photographer,* an oral history interview conducted in 1960 and 1961 by Suzanne Riess (Berkeley: Regional Oral History Office, Bancroft Library, University of California, Berkeley, 1968), p. 188.

6. Ansel Adams, *Born Free and Equal* (New York: U.S. Camera, 1944), p. 25. These photographs and others have been reprinted along with an eloquent "Commentary" by John Hersey, in John Armor and Peter Wright, *Manzanar* (New York: Times Books, 1988). Unlike Lange, Adams was never on the WRA payroll, so his images were not government property. He later donated them to the Library of Congress.

7. They are in Record Group 210.

8. An exception would be photographs, some of them quite grisly, of accidents, suicides, and autopsies.

9. Even more banal were the photographs taken for and by the United States Army. I have in my possession copies of a photograph album compiled for Col. Karl R. Bendetsen, the chief architect of the army's program of initial roundup and incarceration. Some were published in

U.S. War Department, *Final Report: Japanese Evacuation from the West Coast, 1942* (Washington, D.C.: Government Printing Office, 1943).

10. Sylvia E. Danovitch, "The Past Recaptured: The Photographic Record of the Internment of the Japanese-Americans," *Prologue* 12 (1980), pp. 91–103.

11. I have found very little information about Albers, who had been a longtime photographer for the San Francisco *Chronicle*. Lange knew Albers and admired his work. Several of his photographs are reproduced in Maisie Conrat and Richard Conrat, *Executive Order 9066: The Internment of 110,000 Japanese Americans* (Los Angeles: California State Historical Society, 1972), Roger Daniels, *Prisoners without Trial*, and, without proper identification, on the cover of the paperback edition of Roger Daniels, *Concentration Camps, USA* (New York, 1972). Any information about him would be greatly appreciated. Another celebrated former FSA photographer, Russell Lee, was also on the WRA staff during the roundup period, but his images seem to me to be indistinguishable from other WRA images in content, whatever their technical merit may be. Karin Becker Ohrn writes that "several FSA photographers, including [Lange and] Lee documented portions of the evacuation" and that "several" of a number of WRA photographers "had been newspaper photographers," and she lists, without further identification, "Hikaru Iwasaki, Tom Parker, Frank Stewart, Charles Mace, Fred Clark, and Clem Albers." *Dorothea Lange and the Documentary Tradition* (Baton Rouge: Louisiana State University Press, 1980), pp. 122 and 254, fn. 25.

12. There are a number of letters from Japanese American correspondents, many of them written from concentration camps, in the Paul S. Taylor Mss., Bancroft Library, University of California, Berkeley.

13. See Mary W. Hillyer to Paul Taylor, April 23, 1942, Taylor Mss. Other initiators were Alfred M. Bingham, Harry Emerson Fosdick, John Haynes Holmes, James Wood Johnson, Rt. Rev. Msgr. Luigi G. Ligutti, Reinhold Neibuhr, Clarence E. Pickett, Harold Rugg, Norman Thomas, and Oswald Garrison Villard.

14. Paul S. Taylor, "Our Stakes in the Japanese Exodus," *Survey Graphic* 31 (September, 1942), pp. 373–78, 396–97; John J. McCloy to Taylor, May 31, 1942, Taylor to McCloy, December 21, 1943, and Taylor interview, Radio Station KGO, January 13, 1945, all in Taylor Mss. Some Lange photographs illustrate the *Survey Graphic* essay.

15. Auburn (Calif.) *Journal Republican,* January 18, 1945. For a brief account of the 1945 violence, see Daniels, *Concentration Camps, USA,* pp. 158–62.

16. The collaboration between Taylor and Lange, which antedated their marriage, is legendary. Lange, *Making of a Documentary Photographer,* p. 190.

17. Interview of Christina Gardner by Meg Partridge, May 21, 1989, unpaginated transcript in my possession.

18. "I don't at all remember now how it came about that I did this. Who got me into it? It was through someone that I'd worked for in government before, but I don't remember that." Lange, *Making of a Documentary Photographer,* p. 186. Gardner remembered that "Milton Eisenhower, Eisenhower's brother . . . hired Dorothea personally." Gardner-Partridge interview. Conversely, Milton Meltzer writes, without documentation, that "on WRA's staff was an information officer who had shifted over from the Social Security Board Paul Taylor had worked for. When WRA decided it wanted to document its work in photographs, the information man, who knew Dorothea's work, had her appointed to his staff." Meltzer, *Dorothea Lange: A Photographer's Life* (New York: Farrar, Straus & Giroux, 1978), p. 238. One of Eisenhower's biographers, Richard H. Immerman, has told me that he knows of no document connecting Eisenhower and Lange.

19. A Lange photograph of the train at Woodland is reproduced in Conrat and Conrat, *Executive Order 9066,* p. 59.

20. Gardner-Partridge interview. According to Gardner's notes, the first Japanese American shoot was at Mountain View, March 30, 1942.

21. John Modell, ed., *The Kikuchi Diary, Chronicle from an American Concentration Camp: The Tanforan Journals of Charles Kikuchi* (Urbana: University of Illinois Press, 1973), p. 52.

22. Gardner-Partridge interview.

23. Masago Shibuya to Mr. and Mrs. Taylor, March 3, 1943, Taylor Mss. Other letters from her to the Taylors are dated June 20, 1942, December 26, 1942, and August 10, 1943, and one undated letter was obviously written in August 1942.

24. Christina Gardner remembers a woman giving birth at Tanforan: "She lay on a bare table without stirrups and delivered that baby in that horse dung. I mean, there wasn't dung on the floor, but it smelled of it. Those were barely clean, those horse stables, when they moved those people in." Gardner-Partridge interview.

25. Danovitch, "The Past Recaptured," p. 102. Cf. Karin B. Ohrn, "What You See Is What You Get: Dorothea Lange and Ansel Adams at Manzanar," *Journalism History* 4 (1977), pp. 14–22, 32. When Suzanne Riess commented that Ansel Adams found the evacuation justifiable, Lange responded: "That's Ansel. He doesn't have much sense about these things. He was one of those at the beginning of the war who said—they'd had Japanese in their home always as house help and that was characteristic of his household—he said he saw the point. 'You never get to know them,' and all this. He gave the regular line, you know, but he wasn't vicious about it. He's ignorant on these matters. He isn't acutely aware of social change. . . . He felt pretty proud of himself for being such a liberal [laughter] on that book." Lange, *Making of a Documentary Photographer,* p. 190.

26. On Miyatake, see Armor and Wright, *Manzanar,* pp. xvii–xx. A bronze representation of his camera is installed on the sidewalk outside the Japanese American National Museum in Los Angeles's Little Tokyo, which, after dark, flashes some of his images on the museum's outside wall.

Sally Stein

PECULIAR GRACE

Dorothea Lange and the Testimony of the Body

It is by lending his body to the world that the artist changes the world into paintings. To understand these transubstantiations we must go back to the working, actual body—not the body as a chunk of space or a bundle of functions but that body which is an intertwining of vision and movement.

—*Maurice Merleau-Ponty, 1961*

Sentiment and sentimentality, they are difficult concepts to manage.

—*Dorothea Lange, ca. 1960*

Among the many thousands of photographs that Dorothea Lange made are a remarkable number of pictures of feet [5.1]. These are not her most famous pictures, have not been singled out either by the photographer or by critics as notable artistic feats; feet on their own rarely serve such lofty ends.[1] However crude or approximate as pictures, these "footprints" offer a key to what motivated her and her photography.

For most of her life, she limped as a result of a childhood bout with polio, which left her right leg shorter and less developed and her right foot relatively inflexible (and required her as an adult to wear flat shoes that look like children's Mary Janes). Which is not to say she was immobile, far from it. We have only to review the numerous photographs in which she is perched atop cars while focusing her camera to appreciate how active she was.[2] But there are equally many pictures of her resting in a somewhat ungainly, certainly inelegant, sitting or squatting position, with one leg bent at the knee as if to relieve tightness in the hip or lower back [5.2]. That she began to pose like this after making documentary photographs in the South and Southwest of various male figures seeking comfort by squatting, leaning, or sitting with legs sprawled or raised suggests the reciprocal relation photography may encourage between looking and being looked at [5.3].

When asked about her, nearly all of Dorothea Lange's friends and associates would comment on her lameness, though many disagreed as to its import. Her chief biographer, Milton Meltzer, even noted the remarkable variations in the accounts of her lameness and concluded that the condition itself must have varied depending on how tired she was. But lameness, like beauty, or for that matter any other kind of physical difference, may be in the eyes of the beholder; one may be more or less inclined to recognize and respond to it. For example, Willard Van Dyke, one of the first champions of Lange's documentary photography, recalled after her death, "She had a pronounced limp . . . but carried herself so that you were never conscious of it as a handicap."[3] This was meant, one supposes, as a sort of posthumous compliment. She did not make you uncomfortable; she knew how to put you at ease. And this impression Lange seems to have fostered for many years.

Toward the end of her life, however, Lange produced a different picture of herself that was less circumspect and accommodating. In the early 1960s she participated in an extended oral interview; for this kind of private-public record, Lange insisted that there was no getting around the fact of being handicapped; not then, not ever. She claimed it as absolutely central to her identity, as it, she insisted, had claimed her: "I was physically disabled, and no one who hasn't lived the life of a semi-cripple knows how much that means. I think it perhaps was the most important thing that happened to me, and formed me, guided me, instructed me, helped me, and humiliated me."[4]

It is hard to imagine more pointed testimony to the formative, as well as isolating, power of pain, and nearly every essay on Lange mentions her childhood illness and consequent lameness. However, no writer has taken her at her word and pursued the connection between the experience of illness, the effects of physical disability, and the making of the woman and the artist.[5] It is as if the connection produces too much discomfort, has to be downplayed to the point of denial.

When we seek to protect children from something unpleasant, it is often our adult selves that we most want to protect. The social process of denying Lange's handicap became apparent to me when I first saw in a bookshop a version of Meltzer's biography of Lange specially abridged for young readers.[6] For its cover, the juvenile paperback had dispensed with the reproduction of Lange's classic "Migrant Mother" that graced the unabridged hardcover biography, replacing it with an airbrushed drawing of a photographer, yet nothing like the photographer under consideration. Instead it presents a young dreamy blonde with flowing hair and an hourglass figure leaning delicately against a large studio camera, resembling overall some blend of Farrah Fawcett and Cinderella.

The travesty was multilayered. To begin with, the publisher's marketing scheme (it surely was not the author's) made a mockery of the lines by Francis Bacon that Lange held as her credo:

> The contemplation of things as they are
> without substitution or imposture
> without error or confusion
> is in itself a nobler thing
> than a whole harvest of invention.[7]

As for this particular substitution of a "cover girl" image for a photograph of or by Lange, it sought to mask some of the most salient characteristics of Lange's image and identity while conveying a harvest of mixed and wrongheaded messages. It announced to young

5.1.   A Sharecropper's Cabin, Coahoma County, Mississippi, 1937, by Dorothea Lange. U.S. Farm Security Administration, Prints and Photographs Division, Library of Congress, LC USF34 17518-E.

5.2.   Dorothea Lange, 1936, by Rondal Partridge. Private collection.

5.3.   A Park in the Downtown Area, Jacksonville, Florida, July 1936, by Dorothea Lange. U.S. Farm Security Administration, Prints and Photographs Division, Library of Congress, LC USF34 9767-E.

girls (probably fewer boys would read a biography of a woman) that to be a photographer, they still needed to be "pretty as a picture."

In effect, one stereotype, the budding maiden, replaced another in which Lange usually has been cast, the Great Mother.[8] The shift from mother to maiden underscores the few social roles readily available to women, but otherwise this revision adds little to our understanding of Lange and the thematics of her work. To be sure, "Migrant Mother" is her best-known picture, yet it is remarkably ambiguous as commentary on maternity, unless one is predisposed to overlook the utterly compressed composition in which children crowd the mother on all sides [6.16].[9] If "Migrant Mother" stands out as a Depression icon, it also stands out in relation to the rest of Lange's photographs, for she made relatively few other images of the same type. She did not include it or any comparable "madonna" image in her first book, *An American Exodus: A Record of Human Erosion* (1939); and though she did include "Migrant Mother" in her portfolio "The American Country Woman" that she produced in the early 1960s, it appears quite anomalous in that context, for most of the other photographs that she selected depict women independent of family ties.[10] As for the image of Lange as budding maiden who appears to be undecided whether she belongs in front of or behind the lens, we have only to notice in Lange's archive the complete absence of self-portraits—a common genre for novice photographers, particularly female photographers—to appreciate how much she used photography either to deflect attention from herself or to deflect attention from the conventional codes of beauty.

Confining Lange to the madonna-maiden axis reinforces the prevailing view of femininity as a totalizing, monolithic category that blankets (and thus represses) other experiences and positions of social marginality. From a broadened perspective on the diverse social issues that contribute to identity, Lange's work and life serve as testament to the way she perceived difference, less in terms of sexual polarities than in terms of the well and ailing body as it intersected and could be aligned with more conventional forms of difference like class, race, and gender.

Social documentary as it came to be defined in the 1930s tended to situate the individual in relation to his or her immediate environment and community. While Lange publicly subscribed to this idea of documentary and even enunciated one version of it, her photography deemphasized the social and environmental context in order to focus upon the body alone as site of social formation and deformation.[11] The style that she developed influenced other New Deal photographers and came to represent one end of the 1930s spectrum of documentary, arguably the more inviting, accessible end of that spectrum, as it appeared to universalize, perhaps inadvertently, the nature of alienation by embodying it in rather general terms.[12]

Her work is very different from that of another leading thirties documentarian, Walker Evans, and the difference between these two has often been aligned with the poles of gender. The magazine editor Frank Crowninshield noted this difference in the late 1930s when he spoke of Lange's poignancy of feeling and conversely of Evans's cold realism, a distinction that would serve as a recurrent chorus in the documentary discourse.[13] But this warm-to-cool scale is hardly adequate as a means of distinguishing between these photographers. Before translating their photographic work into a gendered discourse of thermal effects, we might consider first the differences in their visual strategies. Evans was a master of geometry, a photographer of architecture who studied it attentively and transferred its rules to the flat photographic plane. Even in his portraiture, the rules of architecture seem to govern the way Evans tightly framed the figure in a vise of built space, a compositional device that may provoke us to consider the material constraints imposed by the environment and the representational constraints imposed by the photographer. Lange, by contrast, tended to dispense with all architecture, or to incorporate the idea of architecture into the body. Indeed, when seeking to explain the way the legacy of illness had marked her sensibility, she sketched out a rough theory of the body's experience as architecture of the self: "We all have those things that form us. They are of what we are built . . . our architecture. And there's much we don't know. I mean this is only a part of it. But the explanation of a person's work sometimes hinges on just [such] a succession of incidents."[14]

Freud wrote more abstractly that the ego is fundamentally a body ego, though at various points he also sought to contain the literal implications of this idea.[15] Lange seemed to hold such an idea dearly and literally. She did not make portraits in the conventional sense of a picture framing head and shoulders that placed emphasis on those features—eyes, brows, forehead—that traditional physiognomy had invested as measures of temperament and intelligence. Instead, she frequently dropped lower to focus on hands in relation to the torso, chest, back, hip, groin, or even lower to focus on the shape and stance of legs and feet. It is as if the body had its own corporeal language to communicate on another frequency with the world and, just as importantly in a body-centered cosmology, with itself.

Though I aim to examine the way Lange's perception of her own body dictated her sense of self and also her vision of, even obsession with, other bodies, I do not mean to reduce Lange's life experience to this single event; that would be to treat illness as an intrinsic stigma, which it need not be. Instead I want to relate this one experience to other events in and around Lange's life that together seem to have shaped her interest in photography and the specific direction it took. Some of these formative events Lange acknowledged, or at least alluded to, in a retrospective account of her development, but she made no public reference to other events that seem just as likely to have influenced her—particularly the charged public discourse relating to the body that surrounded Roosevelt's rise to national leadership in the Great Depression. This essay considers the myriad factors that made the body the central, abiding motif of Lange's work—a motif that served to mediate between her private preoccupations and the more general social issues her photography addressed.

A few biographical details seem especially relevant to her later work. Lange was born in 1895 into a modestly middle-class New Jersey family, though by the time she was an adolescent, the family was in straitened circumstances under the sole support of the mother. At the age of seven, Lange contracted polio, which left her lame in her right leg, though still ambulatory. Five years later, her father left the family under circumstances so painful that she avoided the entire subject with interviewers, close friends, and even with both of her husbands as well as her two sons. In researching her life with the cooperation of her family, Meltzer looked in New York and New Jersey newspapers for evidence of crimes that might have led to his imprisonment or flight. He found nothing.[16] Family members explained to him that she could not bear to discuss the circumstances, which on the one hand suggests the degree of privacy she maintained within her own family, and on the other hand the degree to which she felt personally implicated in her father's disappearance.

Just as many children blame themselves for the divorce of their parents, she may have blamed herself for his departure and even attributed it to her physical handicap: "he would have stayed if I had been whole or healthy" might be the way she would have linked a new trauma in her life to an earlier one. This, of course, is speculation, but it is based on Lange's own accounts of the way her mother and she were locked in a pattern of mutual recrimination.[17]

Absence had the proverbial effect of making the heart grow fonder. Up to the end of her life, Lange recalled her father with some tenderness while she continued to harbor resentment toward her mother, particularly in terms of her mother's handling of her illness.

> *Inwardly my mother had qualities of dependence and the outward appearance of things was very important to her. She had what bothers me in Germans, some kind of a respect for authority that I don't like. When I had polio she used to be that way with doctors, and although I was a little child, I hated it. . . . When I was a growing child and we were out, and some friend was approaching us, she would say to me, "Now walk as well as you can."*[18]

It is a memory of the child being sacrificed for the sake of others and in turn countering with her own rejection; if the child felt that the mother wanted her to conceal her experience, the child sought solace in finding the mother to be lacking in real independence and thus sought to assert her own independence, most immediately from the mother and, more broadly, from the mother's values, "the outward appearance of things."

That she did not spurn the visual but rather channeled it along an unconventional path is indicated by two memories of her teenage years. One is a general recollection of rebelliousness during adolescence, when she made a habit of skipping school to wander about New York City, avoiding her books and instead passing time studying pictures. In addition, she provided one specific visual memory from this period that she readily credited as a turning point.

> *An experience that affected me throughout my life was seeing Isadora Duncan. I saw her every performance that I could. . . . I had never been taken into the upper reaches of human existence before then. . . . It was something unparalleled and unforgettable to many people, not just to myself. But to me it was the greatest thing that ever happened. I still live with that, not as a theatrical performance, but as an extension of human possibility. I saw it there. This woman had a quality that could electrify thousands of people at once by doing nothing really. A minimum of physical motion. My, how strangely she walked. And sometimes she just stood. She was rather sloppy-looking, rather fat, with very heavy upper legs, yet with a peculiar grace, not grace as I had preconceived it, but different.*

She was a person who made a real contribution in that she gave a new form of [to] something. It wasn't based on other dancers' work. You were on unfamiliar ground.[19]

Older, male photographers like Arnold Genthe and Edward Steichen would speak of Duncan in more romantic terms, and their pictures were appropriately honorific, avoiding depicting the performer in too harsh a manner.[20] Though Lange was no less moved by Duncan, it was in a different way. She was less impressed with the way Duncan reconciled the classic and the modern than with the way the performer defied convention, particularly sexual convention, appearing uninhibited by her body's evident age and imperfections, including, as Lange bluntly put it, "very heavy upper legs."

Lange must have identified intensely with this figure, imagining herself capable of achieving grace no matter how strangely she walked. One suspects that she toyed with the idea of taking dance classes (later in San Francisco she would take ballroom dance classes),[21] for she added to her description another of Duncan's troupe performing, "each one so different and all undisciplined. You knew that no one had told them what to do. There was no step, or no count, or any training. It was really in space. Beautiful."[22] This memory, of course, was articulated retrospectively, after Lange had produced her own body of work in which the figure seemed to take off in space. But long before Lange expressed this kind of formal affinity, she had found in Duncan's theatrical presence a model of artistic authority that celebrated the body's idiosyncratic capacity for expression.

Indirectly, it was Duncan who inspired Lange's interest in photography, for within a few years of seeing her on stage Lange had apprenticed herself to the dancer's favorite publicity photographer, Arnold Genthe. From Genthe and a few other studio photographers, she learned the business of theatrical portraiture, but she did not choose to pursue that sort of glamour trade. Rather, as a young woman she behaved more like one of the young Duncan dancers, "all different and undisciplined," for she was determined to chart her own path. At the end of World War I, Lange left New York with the idea of seeing the world. Within a few months, the journey ended in San Francisco, where, lacking money, she used her photographic experience to obtain her first job in a shop that processed photographs. That job was only temporary. In her new environment, Lange displayed considerable enterprise, quickly securing financial backing to set up her own portrait studio. Having established a business and a name for herself by 1920, she married Maynard Dixon, a painter of mythic frontier scenes who at twice her age enjoyed a prominent position in San Francisco's bohemian circle.

During the 1920s, Lange and Dixon had two sons, and following in her mother's footsteps, Lange assumed responsibility for providing her family with a steady income. As for the work she produced in her studio, she would never repudiate it, taking pride in the way it satisfied her clients, but over the course of the decade she became increasingly dissatisfied with its conventionality as well as with the conventionality of her life.

The decade of the 1930s proved to be nearly as formative as her childhood. Though it is certainly possible to detect continuities in her photography throughout her life, it was not until the onset of the Great Depression that her work acquired a consistent sense of purpose, that she became motivated to make art of great social significance. The conditions that make for a productive artist are invariably multiple, and even more complicated is the matter of proportions. In Lange's case, the public and private pressures she experienced in the early 1930s appear so closely interwoven as to dissolve, at least for a time, these categorical distinctions, propelling her to transfer her skill with private portraits and figure studies to the street and from there to hard-hit rural areas.

Referring to the specific factors that contributed to a radical reorientation of her life, Lange later recalled that in the 1920s she felt constrained by her various domestic roles and responsibilities as wife of an established artist and mother of two young sons; by the early 1930s her marriage was unraveling and she separated herself from the role of wife and mother by boarding out her children and establishing a separate residence in her studio. Thus momentous private changes dovetailed with broader social dislocations. On her own for the first time in a decade, she experienced the freedom of "a room of one's own" and with it a sense of single-minded desperation to define herself and her work independently. That business in her portrait studio was slow (as it was for most artists, artisans, and tradespeople in the early 1930s) gave her more time and reason to feel a connection with the unemployed men who congregated in the street below her second-floor studio.

Yet for all these coincidental developments, there still is something remarkable in the fact that she found herself so quickly, establishing almost instantaneously a new direction for her work. Even Lange never ceased to sound amazed when she claimed that the first time she ventured into the street with her camera in the early 1930s, she produced "White Angel Breadline," which became not only one of her most famous pictures but also one of the most oft-reproduced pictures of the Great Depression.[23]

Literally and metaphorically, "White Angel Breadline" [6.13], variously dated 1932 and 1933, is very much a transitional image, sharing the general tenor of uncertainty that characterized the election year of 1932 and the subsequent interregnum between the Hoover and Roosevelt administrations.[24] While the picture centers upon a single figure propped against a railing, the position afforded the viewer is nearly as provisional: neither truly above looking down, nor firmly on the ground at the same level as this figure. Lange had just emerged from her second-floor studio after studying the street from above; she was still so new to street photography that she brought someone along for protection. The picture contains the force of compelling interest combined with a sense of reserve. In her approach to the scene, Lange appears to have stopped for this exposure midway between accustomed and desired points of view, resisting the impulse to probe more closely as the central, destitute figure leans forward in a way that both attracts our attention and blocks our gaze.

From this vantage point, we learn only a little about this figure, certainly not enough to identify him as an individual. His hat is more battered than those behind him; his mouth and hands are both clenched shut, closed gestures echoed by the rim of the cup that rests in the circle formed by his arms. Yet if he appears more archetypal than individual, as a generic figure he is marked as a loner, for all the other signs of retreat that he manifests are summarized in the way he has turned his back on the crowd of men about him.

Already Lange had found a way of capturing social experience in terms of the language of the body rather than of facial expression, thus realizing the special poignancy of the body revealed in a state of isolation. Her good friend, photographer Imogen Cunningham, later recalled that in the 1920s Lange sought to dissociate herself from those who were conspicuously crippled.[25] In the new era of the 1930s, a sense of repulsion turned into attraction to those visibly stigmatized.

Notwithstanding her own accounts of the making of this image—accounts that emphasize intuition rather than deliberate plan or concept—there was a text that guided her preliminary work in the documentary genre. Lange had responded strongly to the season of 1932–1933—so strongly, indeed, that her artist husband, Maynard Dixon, would record in his journal, "Dorothea begins work photographing Forgotten Man," adding to this entry the somewhat envious reflection, "No paintings of this subject."[26] In that year, "Forgotten Man" had become a catchword, set off in capital letters, because it served as the most memorable image in Roosevelt's 1932 presidential campaign. In an April 7, 1932, speech FDR delivered as governor of New York with an eye on the upcoming party convention, he declared, "These unhappy times call for the building of plans . . . that put their faith once more in the forgotten man at the bottom of the economic pyramid."[27] "White Angel Breadline" distilled the final image that the nation had seized upon as a redemptive symbol in Roosevelt's otherwise rather nebulous campaign. In keeping with that symbol, Lange's stress was on the singular man rather than the mass of men, and her photograph even alludes to the position at the bottom of the economic pyramid, as all the action and light move directly down across the wood barricades that ostensibly served to prevent the crowd from spilling into the street.

If Roosevelt's phrase, "the forgotten man," provided an implicit script for Lange in her first foray into the street, her emerging body language developed in response to more than just this particular figure of speech. I have asked her son Daniel Dixon whether she ever expressed personal feelings for Roosevelt, but he rejected the idea, emphasizing that she had no interest in politicians.[28] This may well have been true during most of her life, even during most of the New Deal. Certainly she made few pictures of politicians; most that refer to electoral politics are quite ironic, though one photograph from 1936 of a beat-up Ford bearing a torn Roosevelt campaign sticker on its windshield is more sentimental [5.4, 5.5]. Yet even if she expressed only minor interest in so elevated a personage during most of her lifetime, it is doubtful that she did not respond deeply to FDR at the beginning of his tenure in national politics. For in this same period of general political crisis and transition, Roosevelt's entry into the national political arena briefly turned political discourse in a corporeal direction.

To gain the presidency in 1932, FDR took infinite pains with the representation of his body. A decade earlier at the age of thirty-nine, he contracted polio, a disease that afflicts adults even more severely than children, and he was left permanently paralyzed below the waist. He spent most of the 1920s recovering his strength and trying to learn to walk again before reentering public life. He never succeeded in walking even a few steps without the aid of steel braces. However, before he reentered public life, he mastered the art of appearing to walk with assurance while leaning on family members and other assistants. Roosevelt felt sure that success in politics demanded that he not appear confined to a wheelchair or dependent upon crutch or cane; most certainly he was right on that score, for he proved to be a politician with an uncanny sense of what the public needed to know and what the public could not bear to consider.

5.4.   Campaign Posters in Garage Window, Just before the Primary, Waco, Texas, June 1938, by Dorothea Lange. U.S. Farm Security Administration, Prints and Photographs Division, Library of Congress, LC USF34 18284-C.

5.5.   Windshield of a Migratory Agricultural Laborer's Car, in a Squatter's Camp near Sacramento, November 1936, by Dorothea Lange. U.S. Farm Security Administration, Prints and Photographs Division, Library of Congress, LC USF33 15329-M1.

The image of Roosevelt at the helm but with only limited powers of mobility needed to be deftly managed, requiring what today's political parlance calls a "spin doctor." Roosevelt recognized the liability and sought to address it head-on, though not always with complete candor. He stage-managed stories that suggested he was nearly "cured" of polio; that through swimming he had regained partial use of his legs; that he no longer needed crutches or even a cane; that he hardly noticed the heavy steel braces he required to move even a short distance in a standing position; that his was a small physical handicap that didn't amount to a "hill of beans." *Time* magazine would justify its own controversial description of the president's "shriveled legs" by claiming that no offense could have been produced, given the president's "gallant unconcern," and probably the president took grim pleasure in this sort of callous public rationalization. That he succeeded in projecting an image of resilient recovery was due to his own compensatory efforts to appear inexhaustibly active and in command, as well as to a cooperative press that generally agreed to not depict him as immobilized or confined to a wheelchair (and a forceful staff willing to block the occasional brazen photographer who disregarded this unwritten code).[29]

At the same time, Roosevelt benefitted politically from the general knowledge of the afflictions he had faced and had appeared to overcome. The way he coped with polio served as a test of personal character and public worth. Notwithstanding a background of enormous privilege, he, too, had contended with adversity. Thus he was prepared for the job of guiding the nation through a period of crisis.

The nation assented to this proposition, yet its assent was in part mixed with disavowal. As noted by Hugh Gregory Gallagher, who has produced a particularly insightful study of Roosevelt's physical condition and who also had suffered from polio, many of the men who worked most closely with Roosevelt in the New Deal downplayed his physical handicap to the point of denying that he was crippled, even though his severe impairment was abundantly evident to anyone in his immediate circle.[30]

This desire to confront and simultaneously disavow the nature of his disability Roosevelt skillfully manipulated, perhaps nowhere so subtly as in his first inaugural address. From that speech, most today can only recite one oft-repeated line, "the only thing we have to fear is fear itself"; but the longer passage in which he spoke these words doubtless held his original listeners enthralled for the way it entertained the idea of full disclosure as an antidote to public panic: "This is preeminently the time to speak the truth, the whole truth, frankly and boldly. Nor need we shrink from honestly facing conditions in our country today. This great nation will endure as it has endured, will revive and prosper. So first of all let me assert my firm belief that the only thing we have to fear is fear itself." The phrase did not stop there but continued to elaborate the effects of fear, specifically in terms of immobility and mobility—"nameless, unreasoning, unjustified terror which paralyzes needed efforts to convert retreat into advance."[31] It was a deft way of reminding his listeners who could not see him that he deserved the public's confidence on the basis of his own knowledge of paralysis and his own apparent ability to propel himself forward by sheer force of will.

Even more than the words he employed, or his animated face with its quick grin, jutting chin, and rakishly angled cigarette, there was his voice that resonated with a sense of assurance. That FDR made his voice do double work has been noted by nearly all historians of the period, and it is quite possible that he could not have managed a successful return to politics had it not coincided with the rise of national radio broadcasting. After hearing Roosevelt's inaugural address, Lillian Gish, a veteran motion picture star from the era of silent film, exclaimed that the president seemed "to have been dipped in phosphorus." One historian explains this response in terms of the apparent contrast between the luminous words and the gray blustery weather that shrouded the Washington inauguration on March 4, 1933.[32] Yet one also might interpret these words in terms of the contrast between the projected voice—vibrant, forceful, inviting—and the guarded body.

That the president's somewhat disembodied persona remained an unresolved source of disturbance was indicated by persistent rumors about FDR's physical and mental condition, and less directly in forms of mass entertainment that expressed a mix of fascination and distrust with figures of power whose powers increased in direct proportion to the decline or disappearance of their bodies. One of the first films that appeared after FDR's inauguration, *Gabriel over the White House,* told the story of a president who, after surviving a life-threatening car accident, acquires a new sense of political urgency. He swiftly declares a national state of emergency that permits him to assume absolute authority. A longer-lasting register of uneasiness was the 1930s radio program *The Shadow.* The immensely popular series followed the adventures of an upper-class detective who developed the ability to "cloud men's minds" by "speaking through a filter that made his voice sound distant and distorted." The awesome voice sufficed, enabling the Shadow to circumvent ordinary law in his quest for justice.[33] If these mass-media diversions registered some anxiety, they probably also diverted public anxiety away from Roosevelt, who made such potent use of acoustic effects, for it seems apparent that the public did not really want to comprehend the effort expended in the president's appearance of mastery.

Thus while Roosevelt practiced showmanship, the nation supplied a full house inclined to suspend disbelief. In addition to the relatively mild forms of censorship imposed by the White House was what Gallagher has termed "voluntary censorship," or denial.[34] Yet censorship, like repression, is rarely effective; what is repressed invariably returns in other forms. One cartoon that appeared on the day of Roosevelt's nomination in July 1932 made multiple references to canes and physical infirmity but scrambled the symbols to alter their meaning. The scene presents a neatly constructed Democratic platform behind which stands a jumble of broken planks identified as the GOP platform. The Democratic platform remains unoccupied but supports an armchair, implying that the nominee who mounts it may need to sit. Below the platform stands an expectant male figure, with hat outstretched in one hand while he leans on a cane with the other. But this expectant figure is not Roosevelt. Cartoonist Rollin Kirby deliberately identified him with the generic label "voter." Accordingly, the cane that Roosevelt sought to dispense with in public was transferred from the absent figure of the candidate to the constituents he sought to represent by identifying their pressing social needs. Other cartoonists and graphic artists adopted similar strategies of dissociating the cane from Roosevelt and grafting it onto other figures intended to symbolize the common man, the forgotten farmer, or the down-and-out man on the street.[35] In effect, as the cane was bandied about, passed from one figure to another, the sign of physical infirmity was neutralized, at least partially, converted into a commonplace prop affiliating diverse groups under the institutional rubric of New Deal reform.

FDR's physical condition and the way he represented it predisposed the nation to think of the Depression in pathological terms as a form of paralysis, hopefully of a temporary nature.[36] Yet as metaphor, this image of societal paralysis also circumvented the specifics of the body. Gallagher's revisionist biography of FDR does not broaden its scope to consider how other polio victims responded at the time to seeing FDR succeed in politics while using all the means at his disposal to downplay the extent of his disability. But the phrase he chose as title for his book, *FDR's Splendid Deception,* suggests the way FDR's successful management of his disability may have galled as well as inspired those who knew what it meant to be crippled.

Lange left no verbal record of her response to Roosevelt's efforts to dispel concern about his condition and the various reactions it provoked. She could not have helped being deeply affected by the anxious public reckoning with disability, reminded of her childhood adjustments to a far less severe handicap, the family conflicts that ensued, and the permanent strain it produced between her mother, who sought to maintain appearances, and herself. As an adolescent, Lange had resisted the norms her mother imposed by turning to photography as a way of articulating a separate vision of grace, a separate standard of truth. Again at this juncture in her life, when most Americans found a measure of relief in Roosevelt's supremely adaptive spirit of leadership, Lange found in photography a way of protesting against the belief that personal adjustment to adversity could be so easily accomplished.

Almost immediately after FDR moved to the center of the political arena, she redirected her photography to counter the tendency to imagine the social crisis as generic malady while evading consideration of the actual bodies most affected. If other artists were inclined to convert physical stigmas into social symbols, she worked in contrary fashion to view the trials of the Great Depression as something registered and grappled with first and foremost in the body. Only rarely did Lange focus upon those visibly disabled. If that was too close to home, she used her knowledge of the body's painful limits to insist upon the visceral effects of the Depression by dwelling upon the bodies of those hardest hit by the Depression, whose limited powers depended upon their physical capacities. While Roosevelt put on a happy face to divert attention from his own severe impairment, she resolutely looked to the body for a truth that he was inclined to conceal, dress up, or belittle. She, in other words, looked down, often obliterating the face to avoid any such diversion, offering the viewer the solace of a body disclosed and vulnerable.

In the documentary imagery Lange produced over the course of the 1930s, a recurrent pattern of gestures stands out, constituting a basic set of signs to express the effects of the Depression on the body. One motif, which already had emerged in "White Angel Breadline," is the body that leans, requiring a prop—be it rail, wall, post, or implement—and in this leaning contains the idea, or at least the sense, that the inability to support oneself economically has as its corollary an inability to remain physically erect [5.6, 3.3, 6.12]. A more extreme version of this figuration of dependence appears in her

5.6.   Migrant Agricultural Worker in Marysville, California, Migrant Camp Trying to Figure Out His Year's Earnings, October 1935, by Dorothea Lange. U.S. Farm Security Administration, Prints and Photographs Division, Library of Congress, LC USF34 2533-E.

studies of bodies stunted, crumpled, condensed to grotesquely foreshortened shapes; they tease and test the viewer to find the legs, to see if they are just out of sight or altogether absent, if there remains, to borrow Oliver Sacks's phrase, a leg to stand on.[37] As I study her photographs of men squatting in disheveled clusters, I am reminded of scenes made after battles that provoke a perverse desire to see how exactly the bodies have been mutilated [5.7].

This drama of the figure's tilt, collapse, and revival becomes a choreographic principle of editing in *An American Exodus: A Record of Human Erosion* (1939), the book she produced in collaboration with her second husband, Paul S. Taylor. The choreography is particularly prominent (nearly overwhelming other elements and arguments woven throughout) in the sequence of pictures positioned at the middle of the book. In this central passage, a group of young displaced tenant farmers first appears standing in single-line formation, then appears in broken rank on the ground—self absorbed, evincing no sense of camaraderie—and then is replaced by a lone survivor, a bearded farmer of seventy years who marshals his strength by leaning backward against a fence [5.8, 5.9]. At the very end of the book, this figure long past his prime is echoed by the complementary figure of a female relic of an earlier era. The portrait of Ma Burnham fills the right-hand page, facing a page of her testimony that ends with the salutations she hopes will reach her grandsons in California from her seated, stationary position on the porch of her home in Conroy, Arkansas [5.10].

Before assuming that the emphasis on figures barely able to stand was meant primarily as metaphor, consider Lange's own admission of chronic fatigue. In her extended interview with Suzanne Riess, Lange volunteered: "A few years ago I realized that the entire span of my life I have fought dreadful fatigue. I think I was born tired. . . . I've been tired all my life, every day of my life. I remember when I was only maybe ten years old being as tired as a human being could be, and wishing that I could sleep forever just because I was so tired." Riess sought to translate the admission into metaphors for "world-weariness" and the general effect of the taxing life she had chosen to lead, but Lange rejected these suggestions: "No. It was physical. I think maybe I expended all I had always in one direction or another. That may be some reason why I always knew that I was observing more than I was participating. Maybe I didn't have left what other people had to go on. I don't know what it is, excepting that I know it's been with me, dominant."[38]

It is testimony to her own training to "walk as well as you can," to avoid making others uncomfortable, that Lange seemed hard-pressed to link chronic fatigue to her handicap. Yet this sense of inexplicable physical depletion may well have led her to seek signs of similar exhaustion in others and even, possibly, to amplify those signs as they corroborated her own condition, making her sense of otherness more relative, less absolute and absolutely isolating.

In a few of her photographs from the 1930s, the body is joyously revealed in its capacity to work, to exercise, to enlarge and exhibit its prowess. One such example is her study of a man plowing, his body erect, his muscular back thrown into greater relief by the unusually strong light in which she made this picture.[39] Even more upbeat is another view-from-behind of men who strike jaunty angles as they crowd a fence where they can observe, the caption relates, a ball game [5.11]. But far more often her photographs depict bodies bent out of shape by labor, by prolonged excessive pressure, so that they appear reduced to an overstrained system of levers [5.12, 3.4, 6.14, 6.19].

5.7.　Waiting for the Semimonthly Relief Check at Calipatria, Imperial Valley, California, March 1937, by Dorothea Lange. U.S. Farm Security Administration, Prints and
Photographs Division, Library of Congress, LC USF34 16272-C.

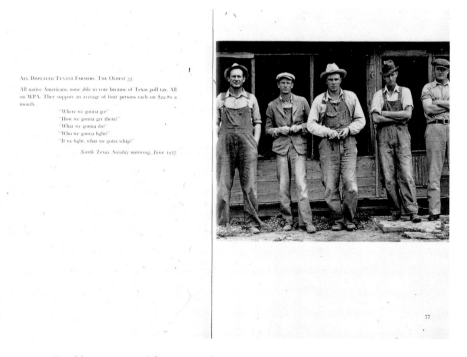

5.8.　Double-page spread from Dorothea Lange and Paul Schuster Taylor, *An American Exodus: A Record of Human Erosion* (New York: Reynal and Hitchcock, 1939),
pp. 76–77.

"Instability and insecurity of farm families leach the binding elements
of rural community life."   [above]
                        —President's Committee on Farm Tenancy, 1937

                                              North Texas, June 1937

Father born in Georgia, mother in Tennessee. Born in Johnson
County, Texas. Age 70. Farmed all his life. Has four children, all farmers. 17 years on this farm, tractored out in 1939. "What will I do? I
don't know. My boys? It's not a question of what they are going to do.
It's a question of what they are going to have to do."   [right]

                                        Hardeman County, Texas, June 1938

5.9.   Double-page spread from Dorothea Lange and Paul Schuster Taylor, *An American Exodus,* pp. 78–79.

MA BURNHAM

My father was a Confederate soldier. He give his age a year older than what
it was to get into the army. After the war he bought 280 acres from the rail-
road and cleared it. We never had a mortgage on it.

In 19 and 20 the land was sold and the money divided. Now none of the
children own their land. It's all done gone, but it raised a family. I've done
my duty—I feel like I have. I've raised 12 children—6 dead, 6 alive, and 2
orphans . . .

                    *   *   *   *   *

Then all owned their farms. The land was good and there was free range.
We made all we ate and wore. We had a loom and wheel. The old settlers
had the cream. Now this hill land has washed. And we don't get anything for
what we sell. We had two teams when this depression hit us. We sold one
team—we had to to get by—and we sold 4 cows.

                    *   *   *   *   *

In 19 and 35 we got only 50 and 60 cents a hundred pounds for picking, and
in 19 and 36 only 60 and 75 cents, and we hoe for 75 cents a day. Then the
government reduced the acreage and where there was enough for two big
families now there's just one. Some of the landowners would rather work
the cotton land themselves and get all the government money. So they cut
down to what they can work themselves, and the farming people are rented
out. They go to town on relief—it's a 'have to' case. Sharecroppers are just
cut out.

Then the Lord taken a hand, and by the time He'd taken a swipe at it there
was drought and army worm. I don't know whether that drought was the
Devil's work or the Lord's work—in 3 days everything wilted.

Folks from this part has left for California in just the last year or so. My two
grandsons—they were renters here and no more—went to California to hunt
work. Those who have gone from here . . . .

If you see my grandsons in California tell 'em you met up with Ma Burnham of Conroy, Arkansas.

                                              June 28, 1938

5.10.   Double-page spread from Dorothea Lange and Paul Schuster Taylor, *An American Exodus,* pp. 150–51.

5.11.   Watching a Ball Game, Shafter Migrant Camp, California, June 1938, by Dorothea Lange. U.S. Farm Security Administration, Prints and Photographs Division,
Library of Congress, LC USF34 19515-C.

5.12. The Son of a Tenant Farmer Hanging Up Strung Tobacco inside the Barn, Granville County, North Carolina, July 1939, by Dorothea Lange. U.S. Farm Security Administration, Prints and Photographs Division, Library of Congress, LC USF34 19998-E.

5.13. Sharecroppers Resting on the Porch after Tobacco Harvest, July 1938, by Dorothea Lange. U.S. Farm Security Administration, Prints and Photographs Division, Library of Congress, LC USF34 18714-C.

Movement, and the stoppage of movement, are primary themes in her work. But there is one recurrent motif that exceeds the conventional idea of motion and its arrest, whereby figures contract inward, refusing to connect with external objects, producing a purely internal circuit. In some, the introverted body appears nearly indecipherable. A picture made in Tilton, Georgia, bears the original, unedited caption "Sharecroppers' harvest in tobacco being over, they are resting, sitting on the porch"; but there is no conventional evidence of recuperation in the scene of one black laborer encircled but isolated from others as he picks at his skin, attentive only to his immediate body, its disturbances and needs [5.13]. She captured the scene in such haste that, like many snapshots, it betrays too nakedly her own interest—in this case, the search for evidence of another's complete preoccupation with his body, so that the world about him appears to be a matter of indifference. The idea in this picture is only roughly realized, the elements too diffused and unbalanced. But at other times Lange would find ways of making pictures that refined the idea of the body as a bounded field of sight, touch, and meaning [5.14]. In these more resolved depictions, the figure appears to fill a vacuum, making contact with nothing but itself, forming signs that compel us as they belong to closed, private fields of communication: barely penetrable, peculiar, yet utterly contained, and thus full of their own invented grace.

There were practical reasons why Lange worked primarily in the countryside in the latter half of the 1930s: her marriage to and collaboration with Paul S. Taylor, an agricultural economist noted for his progressive investigations of rural conditions, and her employment from the mid to late 1930s as a photographer for the Farm Security Administration (FSA). But this shift from city to country also suited her personally and artistically. She later explained the preference in two ways. With people in the countryside, it was easier to make contact, begin conversation, and thus achieve "common ground." Then, too, she noted, there was the challenge that the country people she often encountered were "hard to photograph" since their "roots were all torn out. . . . It's very hard to photograph a proud man against a background like that, because it doesn't show what he's proud about."[40] However, the pictorial evidence suggests that the people whose "roots were all torn out" compelled her *because of* their rootlessness. She identified with that uprooted quality and sought to accentuate it rather than to qualify it.

As for the verbal communication that she found easier to achieve in the countryside, Lange proved to be a talented oral interviewer with an ear for distinctive speech and pithy phrases. But the visual, bodily evidence nearly always took precedence; in the face of any apparent conflict between the expression of the body and the voice, the body, or rather her vision of it, dictated the editing of the words. In her critical study of social documentary photography, Maren Stange demonstrates the extent to which Lange at times radically tailored a caption to orchestrate better the visual and verbal effects. In the case of "Woman of the High Plains," Lange attached to the nearly silhouetted profile the arresting observation, "If You Die, You're Dead—That's All" [5.15]. As it first appeared in Lange and Taylor's *An American Exodus,* the pairing of these seven words with the gaunt female figure whose hands clasp her forehead and neck was so effective that subsequent reproductions of the image usually retain the same text. But this condensation of the woman's statement that Lange had noted is, to put it mildly, wrenched out of context. The bleak view expressed not the woman's own attitude toward life and death but the callous attitude she ascribed to county officials around Childress, Texas, "who provided

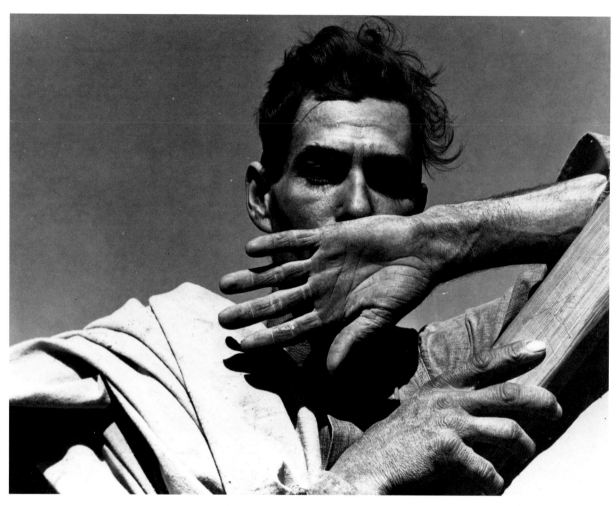

5.14.   Migratory Cotton Picker, Eloy, Arizona, 1940, by Dorothea Lange. U.S. Farm Security Administration, Prints and Photographs Division, Library of Congress.

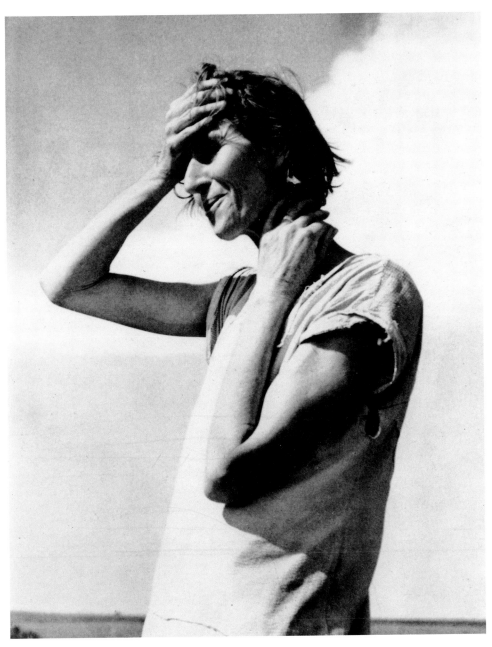

5.15. Woman of the High Plains, Texas Panhandle, 1938, by Dorothea Lange, as reproduced in *An American Exodus,* p. 101.

no relief to those who had been in residence less than a year nor would they bury the indigent." The caption, Stange concludes, serves less to contextualize than to enhance the image.[41] It is a classic demonstration of the way art, or indeed any form of representation, may derive from empathy *and* misunderstanding, with the result that one person's position and outlook is not expressed but is distorted by another. If Lange misread her own record, putting words in this woman's mouth that did not accord with her beliefs, one can understand why; the concise statement distilled the photographer's own vision of a woman who could accept the solace afforded by the limits of her body.

Lange was hardly the only FSA documentary photographer to frame an image and its caption so that it corresponded more closely to the photographer's own vision of truth and beauty. Stange considers the tendency toward esthetic enhancement a general trend in the FSA photography project, and James Curtis has closely reviewed the documentary practices of Arthur Rothstein, Walker Evans, and Russell Lee, as well as Dorothea Lange, for instances of manipulation in order to expose the way these leading social photographers practiced various forms of stage-management while maintaining the fiction of documentary objectivity.[42] But in Lange's case, the imposition may be greater, as her pictures and texts seem to tread on more intimate ground than those produced by her colleagues. As Lange acknowledged at the end of her life, she found that her handicap often enabled her to establish contact with those who had every reason to distrust strangers who appeared more "whole and secure." If she was a representative of an impersonal, distant government (led by a man whose privileges were offset by a handicap that never was fully exposed), she was manifestly on "a different level."[43] On this basis, her subjects may have felt more inclined to open up and collaborate with her, express themselves physically as well as verbally, while she as photographer still controlled the interaction and its outcome.

To the extent that Lange's preoccupation with the body—as site of pain and stigma, of discipline and sensitivity—had very personal sources, we also need to ask why it touched so strong a chord in so large an audience. Such a question may be disposed of neatly by recalling that most traditional art has been valued for its capacity to simplify and thereby convey its message broadly. Lange's photography belongs to that tradition of eloquent simplicity, and accordingly, the resonant appeal of her pictures might be considered decisive proof of her enduring accomplishment as an artist. But this conclusion tends to dodge as much as it explains. There are social dimensions to her kind of artistic economy—an economy that folds a vision of the body politic into the body. Lange's casting of the figure against the sky gave it undistracted space for self-expression, thus avoiding too many social particulars that might restrict identification. This strategy served to generalize those hardest hit by the Depression as more typical, stalwart American individualists. Moreover, in a time of chronic economic stagnation when many faced evictions and many others feared that if conditions worsened, they, too, would face similar prospects, the body as sole, worn housing, for lack of any other shelter, was an especially compelling metaphor.

Decades after the Depression had passed and with it the widespread fears of displacement and eviction, recollections of the era would continue to provoke a "gut reaction." In his oral history of the Depression, Studs Terkel in his emphatic quest for the "personal memoir" uncovered a recurrent tendency among those who had lived through the period to recall their own private anxiety, a memory of chronic depression begat by chronic Depression. Even those who were adamant that they had not internalized their plight, since they recognized the structural forces that caused the massive social dislocations, often sounded as if they were still having to wrestle with the idea of personal accountability, so deeply ingrained was the bootstrap mentality of self-help. Not all agree with this composite diagnosis of the social mentality of the era. Anthony J. Badger reviews the available evidence and reasons quite persuasively that most workers hewed a middle line between indicting themselves and indicting the system. Nevertheless, it is likely that many Depression-era Americans who enjoyed relative comfort still suffered from what Barbara Ehrenreich recently has characterized as the middle-class "fear of falling."[44] Lange's photographs, though they foregrounded those far removed from the seat of power, were made for a middle-class audience, and for herself.

"The secret places of the heart are the real mainsprings of one's actions" was the way, at the end of her life, she tried to explain her most important influences.[45] However conventionally romantic as artist's statement, the assessment may be penetrating while still disclosing little. Throughout her life, she guarded her own secrets fiercely, would never divulge the circumstances of her father's departure, and would rarely acknowledge her own sense of personal stigma. She was not inclined to expose secrets but rather sought to register the enormity of their pressure in and on the body. In her photography, she worked to indicate the force of such withholding while insisting upon the limits of comprehending that which, though it charged the surface, lay submerged beneath it. Some of her most memorable pictures are of gestures that indicate something contained, coiled tightly, simultaneously feared and cherished. In this respect, hers was an art perfectly suited to the taut silence of photography.

NOTES

1. I readily acknowledge that one curator already indicated such a "footpath" through Lange's work. See Therese Thau Heyman's catalogue, *Celebrating a Collection: The Work of Dorothea Lange* (Oakland, Calif.: Oakland Museum, 1978), which opens with one "footprint," the 1930 Wallen "portrait" (O.M. 4030), and includes in the same opening sequence "Mended Stockings, San Francisco, 1934" (O.M. 34024), and which also includes in the closing sequence "Slippers, Korea, 1956" (O.M. 58166) and "Cable Car, San Francisco, 1956" (O.M. 56110). In effect, it is Heyman's selection from the Lange archive that provoked me to reconsider Lange's life and work "from the bottom up." In addition to these pictures that Heyman has published, I have come across at least a dozen more pedestrian views by Lange in a cursory review of the Farm Security Administration (FSA) collection in the Library of Congress.

2. For various views of the photographer at work while balancing her body on the tops of cars, see the photograph of Lange by Rondal Partridge reproduced in Milton Meltzer, *Dorothea Lange: A Photographer's Life* (New York: Farrar, Straus & Giroux, 1978), p. 120, and the series of photographs of Lange by Paul S. Taylor reproduced in Karin Becker Ohrn, *Dorothea Lange and the Documentary Tradition* (Baton Rouge: Louisiana State University Press, 1980), p. 47.

3. Meltzer, *Dorothea Lange: A Photographer's Life,* pp. 7, 76.

4. Dorothea Lange, *The Making of a Documentary Photographer*, an oral history interview conducted in 1960 and 1961 by Suzanne Riess (Berkeley: Regional Oral History Office, Bancroft Library, University of California, Berkeley, 1968), p. 17.

5. The most serious consideration of the issue of Lange's disability is offered by James Curtis, and this brief discussion figures nearly as an afterthought in his essay on Lange's "Migrant Mother." See James Curtis, *Mind's Eye, Mind's Truth* (Philadelphia: Temple University Press, 1989), p. 66. For a more wide-ranging, theoretically speculative essay on the relation between pain and imagining, see Elaine Scarry, *The Body in Pain: The Making and Unmaking of the World* (New York: Oxford, 1985), particularly pp. 161–80.

6. Milton Meltzer, *Dorothea Lange: Life through the Camera* (New York: Puffin/Viking Penguin, 1985), illustrations by Donna Diamond.

7. These lines appear at the beginning of George P. Elliott's essay, "On Dorothea Lange," in the monograph that accompanied Lange's 1966 retrospective, *Dorothea Lange* (New York: Museum of Modern Art, 1966). Elliott adds parenthetically that Lange tacked this quotation onto her darkroom door in 1923 and that the lines continued to serve as a signpost on her various darkrooms until her death in 1965 (p. 6).

8. Andrea Fisher marshals extensive evidence indicating the way Lange was conflated with her most famous Depression-era photograph, "Migrant Mother" (1936)—a conflation that implicitly reduced her artistry to the "natural" terms of maternal identity and affinity. This point extends Wendy Kozol's feminist argument on the importance of the maternal iconography in the crisis of the 1930s when social documentary photography achieved such cultural prominence. However, neither Fisher nor Kozol consider the extent to which Lange's photography often departed from these types, which makes the casting of her and her work in the maternal mold all the more impressive. See Andrea Fisher, *Let Us Now Praise Famous Women* (London: Pandora, 1987), pp. 139–51; Wendy Kozol, "Depictions of Motherhood in Resettlement Administration/ Farm Security Administration Photographs" (Master's thesis, University of California, Los Angeles, 1986); and Kozol, "Madonnas of the Fields: Photography, Gender, and 1930s Farm Relief," *Genders* 2 (July 1988), pp. 1–23.

9. On the conflictual feelings Lange experienced as mother and photographer and the way her ambivalence may be seen to inform the series of photographs she made that resulted in "Migrant Mother," see Curtis, *Mind's Eye, Mind's Truth*, 45–67. In an oblique fashion, Roy Stryker, head of the FSA Historic Section for which Lange worked steadily between 1935 and 1938, acknowledged the ambiguity in "Migrant Mother," which he considered to be his favorite FSA photograph. He marvelled at the emotional qualities of "perseverance . . . restraint and a strange courage" that he found the picture to convey, but he then conceded, "You can see anything you want to in her." Roy Emerson Stryker and Nancy Wood, *In This Proud Land* (Greenwich, Conn.: New York Graphic Society, 1973), p. 19.

10. Lange first exhibited and published parts of a series on the American country woman in 1960. In 1964 she produced a portfolio of her final series, which was published posthumously in book form, with commentary by Beaumont Newhall: *Dorothea Lange Looks at the American Country Woman* (Fort Worth: Amon Carter Museum, 1967).

11. Lange's definitive statement on the subject, "Documentary Photography," was published in *A Pageant of Photography*, the catalog to the exhibition organized by Ansel Adams for the San Francisco World's Fair (1940). However, Meltzer notes that Paul Schuster Taylor, Lange's second husband, helped draft the statement. Meltzer, *Dorothea Lange: A Photographer's Life*, p. 161. In many ways the statement is more consonant with his interests as a sociological economist than with her core work as a social photographer.

12. In "Madonnas of the Fields," Kozol notes the general tendency in FSA photography to isolate figures by positioning them against a low horizon line; to illustrate this point, she refers

to a relatively late FSA photograph from 1941 by Jack Delano (pp. 3–6). If any photographer should be credited with developing this compositional device that became a signature style of New Deal documentary photography, it is Lange, who introduced it to FSA practice in the mid 1930s.

13. T. J. Maloney, ed., *U.S. Camera Annual* (New York: William Morrow, 1939), pp. 11A–12. For subsequent restatements of the same idea, see Fisher, *Let Us Now Praise Famous Women,* p. 140.

14. Lange, *Making of a Documentary Photographer,* p. 18.

15. "The ego is first and foremost a bodily ego; it is not merely a surface entity, but is itself the projection of a surface." Sigmund Freud, *The Ego and the Id* (1923), trans. Joan Riviere, ed. James Strachey (New York: W. W. Norton, 1960), p. 16. The passage is quoted by Oliver Sacks in his self-analysis of the combined effects of a serious physical accident upon his body, body image, and perceptual processes: *A Leg to Stand On* (New York: Harper, 1990), p. 91. However, those less committed to Freud's early interest in neurology cite the passage in his *Interpretation of Dreams* in which Freud proposes to "avoid the temptation to determine psychical reality in any anatomical fashion." See Kaja Silverman, *The Acoustic Mirror* (Bloomington: Indiana University Press, 1988), p. 64.

16. Meltzer, *Dorothea Lange: A Photographer's Life,* p. 8.

17. Ibid., pp. 7–20.

18. Lange, *Making of a Documentary Photographer,* pp. 5–6.

19. Ibid., pp. 60–61.

20. Arnold Genthe, *As I Remember* (New York: Reynal & Hitchcock, 1936), pp. 175–90; Edward Steichen, *A Life in Photography* (Garden City, N.Y.: Doubleday, 1963), Chap. 6.

21. Meltzer, *Dorothea Lange: A Photographer's Life,* pp. 53–54.

22. Lange, *Making of a Documentary Photographer,* p. 63.

23. Interview of Lange by Richard K. Doud, May 22, 1964, p. 5, transcript in Archives of American Art, Smithsonian Institution.

24. In his biography of Lange, Meltzer asserts that the picture was made in 1932, but his chronological evidence is somewhat contradictory on this point. See Meltzer, *Dorothea Lange: A Photographer's Life,* pp. 70–73. One other publication, Dorothea Lange, *Photographs of a Lifetime* (Millerton, N.Y.: Aperture, 1982), also attaches to "White Angel Breadline" the date of 1932, but the monographs by Heyman, Ohrn, and Elliott (the only monograph prepared during Lange's lifetime) all concur on the date of 1933. Notwithstanding this difference in dates, there is no disagreement that the photograph was made in that general period of uneasy political transition between FDR's mounting campaign against the Hoover administration initiated in the spring of 1932 and his assumption of presidential power and institution of emergency reform measures the following spring of 1933.

25. Meltzer, *Dorothea Lange: A Photographer's Life,* pp. 53–54.

26. Ibid., pp. 70–73.

27. Sean Dennis Cashman, *America in the Twenties and Thirties: The Olympian Age of Franklin Delano Roosevelt* (New York: New York University Press, 1989), p. 133.

28. From notes made following my conversation with Daniel Dixon, August 1992.

29. My major source for this material is the revisionist biography by Hugh Gregory Gallagher, *FDR's Splendid Deception* (New York: Dodd, Mead, 1985). On stage-managed stories concerning FDR's health, see p. 84; on the White House's close management of press photographers, pp. 93–94. A subsequent biography, Geoffrey C. Ward's *A First Class Temperament* (New York: Harper & Row, 1989), supports and extends Gallagher's depiction of Roosevelt (pp. 732–94). For an example of the way sympathetic writers helped manage the issue, see Earle D. Looker, "Is Franklin D. Roosevelt Physically Fit to Be President?," *Liberty,* July 25, 1931, pp.

6–10; also [John Franklin Carter], *The New Dealers by an Unofficial Observer* (New York: Simon and Schuster, 1934), pp. 11–12. Roosevelt's reference to the "small physical handicaps that after all don't amount to a hill of beans" is excerpted from a speech he delivered at Warm Springs in 1932, as quoted in *Time,* December 5, 1932, p. 10, the same issue in which the magazine referred to the president-elect's "shriveled legs" (p. 9). *Time's* mirror-to-nature defense of its bald description of FDR appeared in response to various outraged letters from readers that it published (January 2, 1933, pp. 2–4). Two weeks later, the magazine reported that after receiving nearly five hundred letters on the subject, it would close debate on the propriety of its recent coverage (January 16, 1933, p. 2). While the editors claimed that more than half the letters expressed support for the magazine's style of reporting on the president-elect, the magazine thereafter refrained from making similar comments about FDR, though its weekly issues continued to heap scorn on the many other personalities who did not measure up to the editors' yardstick of WASP pulchritude. On the "unregenerately collegiate" style of *Time,* see W. A. Swanberg, *Luce and His Empire* (New York: Charles Scribner's Sons, 1972), p. 122.

30. Gallagher, *FDR's Splendid Deception,* p. 210.

31. Annotated typescript of speech reproduced in Joseph Alsop, *FDR, 1882–1945: A Centenary Remembrance* (New York: Viking, 1982), p. 115.

32. Michael E. Parrish, *Anxious Decades: America in Prosperity and Depression, 1920–1941* (New York: W. W. Norton, 1992), p. 289.

33. On *Gabriel over the White House,* see Andrew Bergman, *We're in the Money* (New York: Harper, 1972), pp. 115–20. Sean Dennis Cashman offers a thumbnail description of the fully evolved "Shadow" in *America in the Twenties and Thirties,* pp. 321–22. The debut of *The Shadow* on radio preceded FDR's entry into national politics, but the detective metamorphosed during the first half of the 1930s from a more ordinary gumshoe to a sleuth with fantastic powers of vocal manipulation. This metamorphosis is traced in J. Fred MacDonald, *Don't Touch That Dial* (Chicago: Nelson-Hall, 1979), pp. 171–83.

34. Gallagher, *FDR's Splendid Deception,* pp. 94–97.

35. Regarding generic images of physical dependency that coincided with FDR's emergence on the national political scene, in addition to Kirby's cartoon "Comparative Workmanship," published in the New York *World Telegram* on July 2, 1932, see also Charles MacCauley's "A Message of Hope," New York *Mirror,* July 4, 1932 (though the farmer in this scene is supported by his wife rather than by cane or farm implement), and Carey Cassius Orr's "The Crop Outlook," Chicago *Daily Tribune,* July 6, 1932, p. 1. For an urban variation on this same theme, see Miguel Covarrubias's October 1933 cover of *Vanity Fair,* featuring two silhouetted figures cut from stock-market quotation pages: a corpulent, high-hatted, cigar-smoking figure bearing the date stamp "1929" faces a rumpled and emaciated silhouette, branded "1933," whose most prominent attribute is the crutch he carries.

My review of cartoons from the New Deal era that incorporate yet generalize the idea of physical dependency was provoked by numerous scholarly references to another cartoon from July 1932 attributed to Kirby; but an extensive search for it has turned up nothing, leading me to wonder whether it ever existed except in subsequent histories of the era. One political associate and early biographer of FDR recalled in the 1950s that the first cartoon to hail Roosevelt after his nomination was an image of a farmer leaning on a hoe while looking skyward as a plane flies overhead sporting the slogan "New Deal." Samuel I. Rosenman, *Working with Roosevelt* (New York: Harper, 1952), p. 78. The historic source for such an image is Jean-François Millet's painting *Man with a Hoe* (1860–1862), and already in Millet's painting the hoe served double duty as implement and crutch for a laborer arrested by fatigue. If Rosenman was relying on memory (and his papers at the Franklin D. Roosevelt Library include no such cartoon), he may have conflated some of the above graphics along with quite prominent verbal references in 1932 to the turn-of-the-century poem by Edwin Markham based on the Millet painting. See Gilbert Seldes, *The Years of the Locust* (Boston: Little, Brown, 1933), p. 256.

Surely the significance of Millet's revival in this period demands further study, especially as it coincided with the emergence of a genre of social photography that featured rural life and labor. But if the elusive New Deal cartoon based on *Man with a Hoe* proves to be a phantom image, it is worth speculating why references to it have continued to appear in histories of Roosevelt and the New Deal, even though none reproduces it. See Frank Freidel, *Franklin D. Roosevelt: The Triumph* (Boston: Little Brown, 1956), p. 315; James MacGregor Burns, *Roosevelt: The Lion and the Fox* (New York: Harcourt, Brace, 1956), p. 140; Kenneth S. Davis, *FDR: The New York Years, 1928–1933* (New York: Random House, 1979), p. 335; Nathan Miller, *FDR: An Intimate History* (Garden City, N.Y.: Doubleday, 1983), p. 279. In the historical imagination, these rehearsals may still satisfy a need to speak of crutches while avoiding pinning them directly, or exclusively, on the president.

36. The metaphor persisted for at least a decade. See, for example, Lewis Browne, *Something Went Wrong* (New York: Macmillan, 1942), p. 304.

37. Sacks, *A Leg to Stand On.*

38. Lange, *Making of a Documentary Photographer,* p. 73.

39. See "Spring Plowing, Cauliflower Fields, Guadalupe, California" (1936), in Lange, *Photographs of a Lifetime,* p. 26.

40. As quoted in Meltzer, *Dorothea Lange: A Photographer's Life,* p. 97, though his source for the quotation is not documented.

41. Maren Stange, *Symbols of Ideal Life* (New York: Cambridge, 1989), pp. 119–23.

42. Curtis, *Mind's Eye, Mind's Truth.*

43. Lange, *Making of a Documentary Photographer,* pp. 17–18.

44. Studs Terkel, *Hard Times* (New York: Pantheon, 1970), especially pp. 44–49, 78–81; Anthony J. Badger, *The New Deal: The Depression Years, 1933–1940* (New York: Noonday, 1989), pp. 38–41; Barbara Ehrenreich, *Fear of Falling: The Inner Life of the Middle-Class* (New York: Pantheon, 1989).

45. Lange, *Making of a Documentary Photographer,* p. 216.

DOROTHEA LANGE

Her Words and Images

6.1. Consie on Horseback, ca. 1920

I had in my early years, before I was fully grown, a great many things to meet, some very difficult, a variety of experiences that a child shouldn't really meet alone. I was aware that I had to meet them alone, and I did.[1]

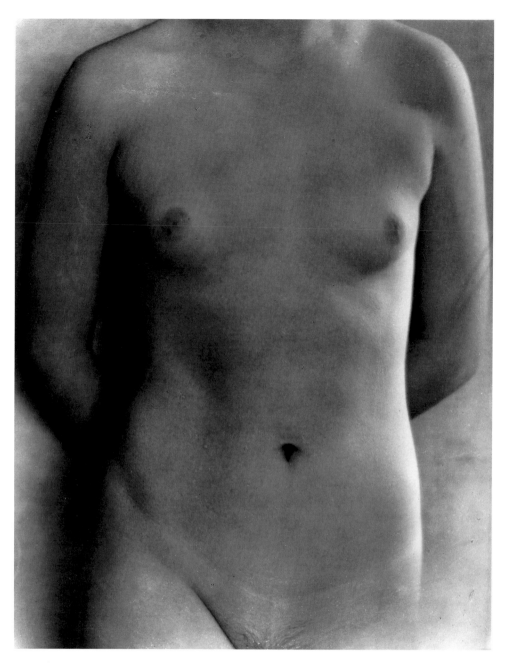

6.2.   Torso, San Francisco, 1923

My home at that time was Hoboken. We had gone back there to live with my grand-mother. We had to. My mother had to hold things together; my father abandoned us.[2]

There were two days a week when my mother worked nights and I went home alone. I went home generally about five o'clock, along the Bowery. I remember how afraid I was each time, never without fear. I knew how to keep an expression of face that would draw no attention, so none of these drunks' eyes would light on me.[3]

Then also I was physically disabled, and no one who hasn't lived the life of a semi-cripple knows how much that means. It formed me, guided me, instructed me, helped me and humiliated me. All those things at once.[4]

6.3.   My Mother, the "Wuz," 1920s

My mother had qualities of dependence and the outward appearance of things was very important to her. She had some kind of a respect for authority that I don't like. When I had polio she used to be that way with the doctors, and although I was a little child, I hated it.[5]

Yet I made a photograph of her, which is through and through my mother, and it reveals that I loved her very much.[6]

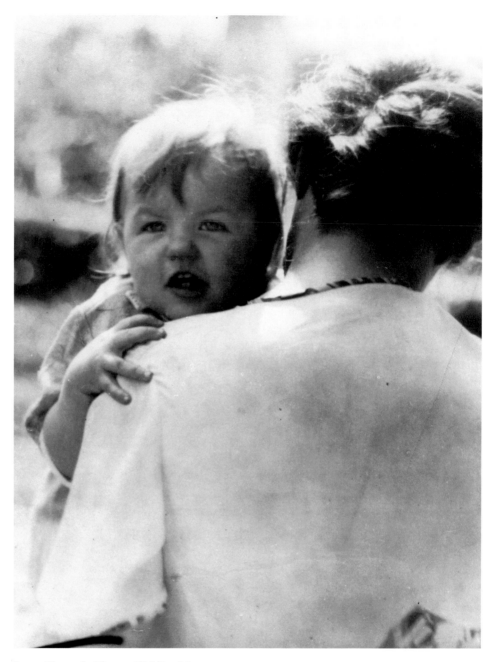

6.4.   Gertrude Clausen Holding Nancy, 1932

I came to California in 1918.[7] I was a portrait photographer in San Francisco. I struggled hard with it, and some of my longest, hardest working years were those years, up to the limit of my strength. It was quite a venture because it was a rather expensive place, and I had what they called the cream of the trade.

6.5.   Roi Partridge Portrait, San Francisco, 1925

I enjoyed every portrait I made in an individual way, but it wasn't what I really wanted to do. I wanted to work on a broader basis. I realized I was photographing only people who paid me for it. That bothered me.[8]

6.6.   Maynard Dixon on Wall, 1920s

I was married in the meanwhile [to Maynard Dixon.]? I have never watched any person's life as closely, up to that time, as I watched his, what it held, how he lived it. He was at that time forty-five years old, and I was twenty-one years younger.[10]

I had energy and health in those days. I had a family to hold together, and two little boys to rear without disturbing [Maynard] too much, though he was very good to us. But it was sort of myself and the little boys, and he. It wasn't so much he and I, and the little boys. I thought I was protecting him, helping him in his work.[11]

But I wasn't really involved in the vitals of the man, not in the vitals.[12] *All the years that I lived with him, which were fifteen years, I continued to reserve a small portion of my life, and that was my photographic area.*[13]

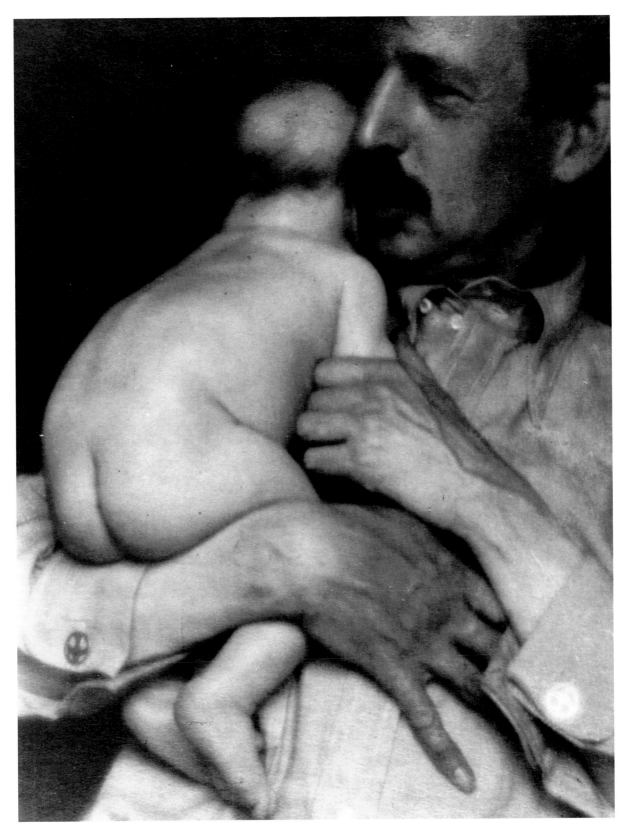

6.7.   Maynard and Son, 1920s

6.8.   Hopis on Trail to Plaza, 1920s

6.9.   Woman and Chickens, Taos, New Mexico, 1931

San Francisco was [Maynard's] base, and he would go on sketching trips.[14] I went on one in 1923 to Arizona and we were gone four months.

We went into a country which was endless and timeless, and way off from the pressures that I thought were part of life. The earth and the heavens, even the change of seasons, I'd never really experienced until that time. Then I became aware.

On the second trip we were gone two months and we were camped at the base of Walpi Mesa.[15]

6.10.   Southwest, 1920s

The third trip was in 1930 or 1931 when we lived in Taos, New Mexico, for eight months with the two little boys [Dan and John]. We weren't there because of the Depression but because Maynard wanted to paint and there was enough money to see us through. The outside world was full of uncertainty and unrest and trouble and we got in that car and we went and stayed there.[16]

6.11.   Navaho Mother and Child, 1931

6.12.   Waiting for Semimonthly Relief Check, Imperial Valley, California, 1937

When we came back [to San Francisco] we were confronted immediately with the terrors of the Depression. Everyone was so shocked and panicky. No one knew what was ahead.[17]

I was compelled to photograph as a direct response to what was around me.[18] *I went out just absolutely in the blind staggers.*[19]

6.13.   White Angel Breadline, San Francisco, California, 1933

I was just gathering my forces, and that took a little bit because I wasn't accustomed to jostling about in groups of tormented, depressed and angry men with a camera.[20]

6.14. Mexican Grandmother Harvesting Tomatoes, California, 1938

6.15.   Field Worker's Home by a Frozen Pea Field, California, 1937

Paul Taylor, who was a professor at the University of California, telephoned me. He had a grant from the State of California to investigate agricultural labor and he wanted photographs as visual evidence to accompany it.

Well, a way would have to be found and a way was found. My papers were made out as a typist because they'd just roar back if you mention photographer.

But that was the way I got started. I worked for the California State Emergency Relief Administration. And the next thing I knew, I was married to [Paul Taylor].[21]

6.16. Migrant Mother, Nipomo, California, 1936

6.17.   Looking for Work in the Pea Fields, California, 1936

That work led to the appointment in the Farm Security Administration. I was asked whether I could work in California but with a federal connection. In the early days of the New Deal all manner of unprecedented things were done and they found a way.[22]

6.18.   Planting Cantaloupe, Imperial Valley, California, 1937

6.19.   Bindlestiff, Napa Valley, California 1938

No one was ever given exact directions. You were turned loose in a region, and the assignment was more like this: "See what is really there. What does it look like, what does it feel like? What actually is the human condition?"[23]

6.20.   Undernourished Cotton Picker's Child, Kern County, California, 1938

When you are doing a lot of hard fast field work, it's a physical necessity to forget
every day. You can't try to remember it in any continuity. You get so burdened if you
try to do it the other way. You can't dictate to your material, you have to follow this
kind of material. You miss it.[24]

    We found our way in, slid in on the edges. We used our hunches. And it was
hard, hard living. It wasn't easy, but you didn't ever quit in the middle of anything
because it was uncomfortable.[25]

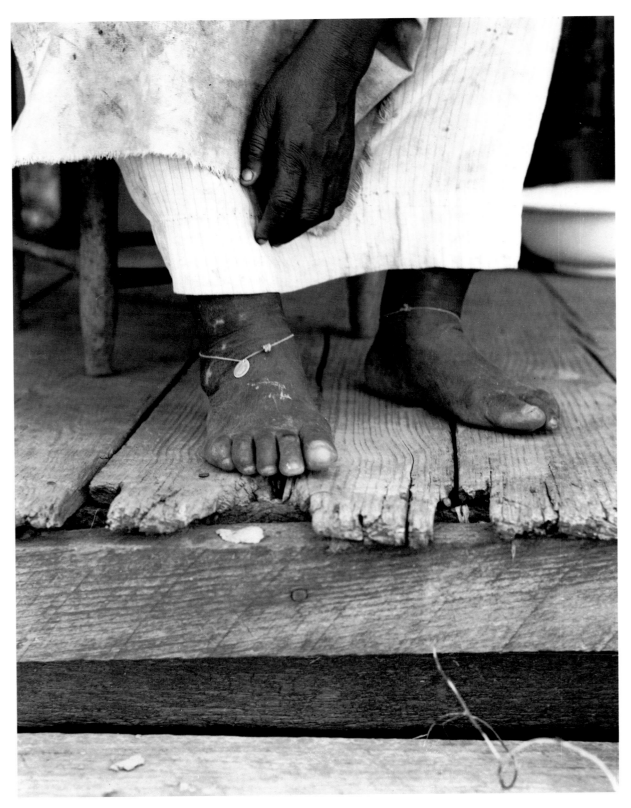

6.21. Fifty-Seven-Year-Old Sharecropper Woman, Mississippi, 1937

6.22.   Man on Farm-All Tractor, Childress County, Texas, 1938

I didn't know a mule from a tractor when I started. I got interested in the way in which [agriculture] was being mechanized. What I see now is the mechanization has brought about enormous problems.

There is no place for people to go to live on the land any more, and they're living. That's a wild statement, isn't it? And yet, it begins to look as though it's true in our country. We have, in my lifetime, changed from rural to urban. In my lifetime, that little space, this tremendous thing has happened.[26]

6.23.   Never Been Out of Mississippi, 1936

6.24.   Cafe, Richmond, California, 1942

6.25.   End of the Shift, Richmond Shipyards, 1943

In 1939 the war started.[27] *The war brought money and brought a way out. The pay-checks came in. Everyone was working, there was overtime and swing shifts and graveyard shifts. The migratory workers settled down, and slept under a roof and the Negroes kept coming, leaving the cotton fields of the South. Everyone was welcome.*[28]

6.26.   Richmond, California, 1942

In 1942 I worked for the War Relocation Authority. I photographed the billboards that were up at the time. Savage, savage billboards.

I photographed the evacuation of the Japanese, the Japanese Americans from the Bay Area.[29] I photographed their arrival in the assembly centers. And then they were moved again, into the interior.[30]

6.27.   One Nation Indivisible, San Francisco, 1942

6.28.   Manzanar Relocation Center, 1942

6.29.   Grandfather and Grandson, Manzanar, 1942

I photographed only one of the interior centers, Manzanar, in Owens Valley.[31] *They had the meanest dust storms there, and not a blade of grass. And the springs are so cruel; when those people arrived there they couldn't keep the tar paper on the shacks. Oh, my. There were some pretty terrible chapters of that history.*

I was employed a year and a half to do that, and it was very, very difficult.[32] *This is what we did. How did it happen? How could we?*[33]

6.30.   Man with Sledgehammer, 1951

1945, that's when I got sick. And then 1946, total loss. Here in 1946, Peralta Hospital, ulcers, doctors, doctors. [I was] on the operating table and the doctor was there. He was going to operate on my throat and there was a telephone call. The doctor took it and he said, "It's for you." And I picked it up and what I heard was [my son] Dan's voice, and he said, "Dad is dead." And he hung up.

6.31.   Pickets on Market Street, Western Union Telegraphers Strike, May 1952

I said, "I'm sorry, doctor, I've got to go home." I got up and went home. That was that.[34]

The next nine years, as far as work is concerned, I have almost nothing. I have serious limits health-wise, and there's no way out of it.[35]

6.32.   Church Service, Toquerville, Utah, 1953

6.33.   Gunlock, Utah, 1953

In '53 I went to Utah on a Life *assignment.*[36]
     This is a town that has no neon lights yet. It's just a little pocket of early American life, still isolated.[37]

6.34.   Hands, Two Boys and Grandfather, Ireland, detail, 1954

6.35.   Cattle Day in Ennistymon Market, Ireland, 1954

In 1954, I got to Ireland.[38] *Of course, Ireland is always contrary.*[39]

6.36.   Patrick Flanagan Selling Sheep, Ireland, detail, 1954

6.37.   Irish Child, 1954

But once in a while the whole earth smiles for a minute, and then it's different.[40]

6.38.   Egyptian Shepherd Boy, 1963

In 1958 I went on a trip around the world, and I said to the doctor, "Should I go?,"
and he said, "What's the difference whether you die here or there? Let's go!"[41]

6.39.   Palestinian Child, 1958

6.40.   Korea, 1958

Can Asia be photographed on black and white film? I am confronted with doubts as to what I can grasp and record on this journey. The pageant is vast, and I clutch at tiny details, inadequate.[42]

I lie awake on my bed at night and listen to the sound of this old-walled city, as it settles into silence. There are no street lights and there is curfew at midnight. Silence then falls like a curtain after that sound. There is finally from the depth of the night one crier left. He seems to wander in and out of the streets surrounding this hotel, for I now know his voice well. He sounds like a lone wild animal out of Manchuria. Somehow he reminds me of the long, long past year. I wish I could remember what that song is.[43]

6.41.   Vietnamese Mother and Child, 1958

6.42.   Egyptian Village, 1963

I'm always pushing in many directions at once, always trying to overreach myself. It keeps me constantly restless, and probing and fractured.

However, that way of working engenders a very good kind of fatigue, because it keeps you alive. You may be exhausted by the complexities of your existence, but there is no retreat in it. You are right out on the thin edge all the time, where you are unprotected and defenseless.[44]

6.43.   Egyptian Woman in Doorway, 1963

6.44.   Veiled Women, ca. 1963

The bazaars of Peshawar are extraordinary in that they really exist here, today, and that we can move down their crowded, narrow, jostling, noisy streets, looking into these dark faces, all men, remember, almost no women abroad, between all manner of wares, festooned over head, on the sidewalk underfoot, with camel trains and donkey carts and horse-drawn tongas and mud and silks, and furs and coarse thick blankets, samovars, dark eyes under wool caps (like Erasmus, Paul said), gold shoes, gleaming copper, red apples and the evening smoke and cold descending and the lights on in the stalls. All so close to the visitor, and yet so remote.[45]

6.45.   Pathan Warrior Tribesman, Khyber Pass, 1958

6.46.   Egyptian Farmer, 1963

Last night during the night, the sky without a glimmer of light (it was about 4 a.m.), I heard men singing in what sounded like a procession. Utter stillness and blackness. And this deep well of sound which stirred the air and hung there. It passed, and I listened to the voices grow more faint, then it was still again.

6.47.   Procession Bearing Food to the Dead, Upper Egypt, 1963

How, in my life, have I listened to night sounds. The Euclid streetcar which didn't stop to bring Dan back and under the roof. The streetcars and the blind man, during those hot nights at the Chosun Hotel in Seoul. The first sounds of morning in Vinh Long. Then this last night, in this desert city, was the most beautiful singing that ever I have heard.[46]

6.48.   Woman on Stairs, Indonesia, detail, 1958

6.49.   Friend and Neighbor, 1944

I sit in the kitchen. Three months we have been home. I am waiting for the potatoes to be done; I have a head full of this and that, how to manage, what to do, details of everything, work undone, tensions and splinters. A clear high sweet sound reaches me, and fills me. A little bell. There it is, under the dark and dreadful eaves where we hung it, hoping that the winds of the Pacific would make it sing of that glittering Sunday morning in the miraculous temple of Bangkok.

The sound is faint, but clear.

Hello and goodbye to Bangkok, I say, as the potatoes finally boil.[47]

6.50.   Gregor Running to the Park, 1955

6.51.   The Kitchen Sink Corner, Summer, 1957

I would like to have one year. Just one, where I would not have to take into account anything but my own inner demands. Maybe everybody would like that, but I can't.[48]

6.52.   Andrew at Steep Ravine, 1957

In the last two weeks time has stood still. I now know that I shall not recover as I have been able to so many times before, for I have an inoperable and incurable cancer of the esophagus, and the way ahead is unchartable.[49]

6.53.   Paul Carrying Lisa, 1962

6.54.   Bad Trouble over the Weekend, 1964

6.55.   Andrew, Berkeley, 1957

Now, at a time when I have such feeble energies, I could do my best work, I know.[50]

6.56.   Paul, Briefcase, and Umbrella, 1957

6.57.   Trees, Berkeley, 1957

I have not yet been able to break the habit of thinking that everything is ahead. That has been my lifelong attitude. I find that every day taken separately, with full weight given to each hour, has seen me through these last months, and in some ways it has been a great time.[51]

NOTES

Editor's note: To make the quotations easier to read, I have not followed the convention of adding ellipsis points where I have left out words or sentences. Most of the sources I used are audio recordings, which can be quite digressive.

1. Dorothea Lange, *The Making of a Documentary Photographer,* an oral history interview conducted in 1960 and 1961 by Susan Riess (Berkeley: Regional Oral History Office, Bancroft Library, University of California, Berkeley, 1968), p. 11.

2. Ibid., p. 12.

3. Ibid., pp. 15–16.

4. Ibid., p. 17.

5. Ibid., pp. 5–6.

6. Ibid., p. 6.

7. Ibid., p. 78.

8. Interview of Dorothea Lange by Richard K. Doud, May 22, 1964, transcript in Archives of American Art, Smithsonian Institution, p. 57.

9. Ibid.

10. Lange, *Making of a Documentary Photographer,* p. 97.

11. Ibid., p. 102.

12. Ibid., p. 123.

13. Ibid., p. 97.

14. Ibid., p. 121.

15. Ibid., p. 126.

16. Ibid., p. 136.

17. Ibid., p. 141.

18. Ibid., p. 145.

19. Ibid., p. 147.

20. Ibid., p. 149.

21. Ibid.

22. Ibid.

23. Film script for "Dorothea Lange: A Visual Life," Meg Partridge, Pacific Pictures, Valley Ford, Calif., pp. 5–6.

24. Film script, p. 7.

25. Lange-Doud interview, p. 65.

26. Ibid., pp. 71–72.

27. Outtakes from the interviews of Dorothea Lange, 1963–1965, held in her home at 1163 Euclid Avenue, Berkeley, Calif., for two films produced for National Educational Television by KQED, Inc., San Francisco (*Closer for Me* and *Under the Trees*), tape 22, p. 449. Copyright and all other rights held by Dorothea Lange Collection, The Oakland Museum, gift courtesy of Robert Katz and Paul Schuster Taylor.

28. Film script, p. 9.

29. Ibid., pp. 11–12.

30. Lange, *Making of a Documentary Photographer,* p. 188.

31. Ibid.

32. Ibid., p. 191.

33. Film script, p. 12.

34. Outtakes, tape 22, p. 446.

35. Lange, *Making of a Documentary Photographer,* p. 153.

36. Outtakes, tape 22, p. 452.

37. Outtakes, tape 14, p. 310.

38. Outtakes, tape 22, p. 446. Lange erroneously says she was there in 1955, but her photos are dated 1954.

39. Film script, p. 15.

40. Ibid.

41. Ibid.

42. Dorothea Lange's Journal, Saigon, Vietnam, September 24, 1958, Oakland Museum, Oakland, Calif.

43. Ibid., Seoul, Korea, July 23, 1958.

44. Film script, p. 19.

45. Dorothea Lange's Journal, Pakistan, December, n.d., 1958.

46. Ibid., Pakistan, December 8, 1958.

47. Ibid., Berkeley, Calif., n.d.

48. Lange, *Making of a Documentary Photographer,* p. 219.

49. Lange to Beaumont Newhall, September 15, 1964, Beaumont Newhall Estate, Santa Fe, N.M.

50. Lange, *Making of a Documentary Photographer,* p. 218.

51. Lange to Beaumont Newhall, July 29, 1965, Newhall Estate.

SOURCES

Figs. 6.4, 6.6: Private collections.

Figs. 6.12, 6.14, 6.15, 6.16, 6.17, 6.18, 6.19, 6.20, 6.21, 6.22, 6.23: U.S. Farm Security Administration, Prints and Photographs Division, Library of Congress. The Library of Congress holds all of Lange's work for the FSA.

Figs. 6.26, 6.27, 6.28, 6.29: Still Picture Division, National Archives. The National Archives holds the negatives for all of Lange's internment photographs, made for the War Relocation Authority (WRA).

Remaining figs.: Dorothea Lange Collection, the Oakland Museum, Oakland, Calif. All of Lange's work, except for her government work, is held at the Oakland Museum. It also has copy negatives of some of her FSA and WRA work, and has graciously provided the prints for Figs. 6.16, 6.22, 6.26, 6.27, and 6.28.

7

ANSEL ADAMS REMEMBERS DOROTHEA LANGE

An Interview by Therese Heyman

Dorothea Lange's contemporaries play an important part in how we know and experience Lange today. When I undertook to organize the major traveling exhibition of Lange's work, *Celebrating a Collection* (1978), I wanted to get a firsthand account of her as a working photographer. I therefore turned, in 1976, to Ansel Adams, probably Lange's most accomplished collaborator.

Adams was unique in Lange's circle; he had shared seven assignments with her when they were both employed by the Office of War Information (OWI). He had a wide experience of collaboration and working relationships with other photographers, which gave him a generous perspective.

Lange and Adams treated each other with a respect that each had earned under equal terms. And each seemed to want something only the other could offer. In a 1962 letter to Adams, Lange protests a lapse of contact: "Silence between you and me can last just so long, and then I feel the need to reach out toward you and say, Hello, are you there? Is all well with you?"

In September 1976, Ansel and I sat together in the bay window of his Carmel home, looking out at the clear, dramatic view of the waves breaking on the rocky shore below. Ansel rewarded me with a lively account of his friendship with Dorothea Lange.

He identified three stages in Lange's approach to people: the social "hello," followed immediately by a formidable proving of herself as the intense, ever-working professional in control of many facts and many answers. Later, the human and somewhat more flexible photographer would emerge. Ansel also offered a view of Lange from outside the university community, where she deferred to her husband, Paul Taylor, and his colleagues, who were mostly trained speakers and intellectuals. Lange's photographer friends, by contrast, seldom strayed into social theory; they tended to remain within their firsthand, anecdotal experiences. They did not measure the drift of the economy or rates of unemployment, nor did they know what Marxist theory promised or what it delivered. In that setting, Ansel noted, Lange gave her opinions freely, without feeling the constraints imposed in the company of Berkeley academics.

Although Lange did not write often of her busy and at times even harried life with Taylor, we know that she managed a household for her two young sons and Maynard Dixon's daughter, and accommodated visits from Taylor's son and his sisters—all this during the time she was traveling, following Resettlement Agency scripts, and sending budgets, negatives, and prints back and forth to Washington D.C. Reflection and considered political statements were therefore not likely elements in her mode of expression, but her work demonstrates that she responded intensely to what she saw and thought about the field.

We are fortunate to have Ansel Adams's vivid recollections and unique overview to add to the wealth of the heritage that Lange has left us.

ANSEL ADAMS: I knew [Dorothea] when she was married to Maynard [Dixon]. . . . Dorothea had done some Navajo Indian portraits, I think—Navajo or Hopi—and she was quite a pictorialist. When the f64 group concept originated in 1930 or 1931 . . . she was not included, which upset her very much, I found out later. It was one of these strange things where the character of her work wasn't acknowledged. . . . There wasn't much that I knew about Dorothea or her work until of course the first big episode, the general strike [1934].

I did a series of pictures in 1930 for Paul Taylor,[1] [of] the Mexican laborers over in Fresno. They came out in the *New Statesman.* . . . Then she and Paul became . . . interested in labor. This was the beginning of the Depression—and I'm trying to put the dates together, how this first came about. The general strike as I remember was the turning point. Dorothea was very active and there was a picture she'd made of a breadline which I was terribly impressed with and used [in my book] *Making a Photograph.* . . . Still, her style was not along the lines of the f64. . . . We made a mistake because I think if we'd . . . really made an effort to find out what she was trying to do, we would have found out that she was really tremendously interested in photography as such, but it took a catastrophe to bring it out. Then she tried to get Maynard to paint the scenes of the strike . . . and the breadlines, and that wasn't Maynard's dish of tea at all. . . . The next thing I knew she had left Maynard and had married Paul Taylor.

I don't know the interval of time. Then we became good friends, and I developed a lot of her negatives for her that she did down in the South.[2] She sent film packs to me in Yosemite. They'd still come smelling of mildew. You have no idea of the heat. It was August, you know, in the South on the farms and all this damp and you'd open this packet and, euuu, you just smelled marshes and whew . . . some of them were damaged by humidity.

THERESE HEYMAN: How did you happen to make that arrangement? It seems unique to me. I mean I think it was inspired of Dorothea to ask you.

AA: She said, "What am I going to do? I don't want anybody else developing my negatives, and I don't know how I'm going to go down there six weeks to a month, can I send them to you for keeping?" I said I'd be delighted to do it, but it's much better if I develop them because they're all fogged up with humidity and mold and just keeping them in a cooler place isn't going to help. So we had this system at Yosemite with deep tanks so I could take a whole—two, three film packs at a time—and they were quite well developed and very consistent. I must have done thirty packs. Anyway, a terrific number.

TH: Do you remember anything about the negatives themselves? There's been a lot of criticism of those negatives, Ansel, that they were muddy, gray.

AA: Well, it was a muddy and gray situation. The film was broken down. I mean, obviously it had suffered heat. In those days the film wasn't sealed as it is now and, let's see, I can remember now the first several I developed seemed flat and so then I developed them more and that really didn't help. It was obvious that the conditions must have been rather ghastly. But I remember they were on the flat side, misty and heavy, very strange. There were some brilliant ones, I remember that. Some details of architecture and portraits of people. But the ones outside were very bad . . . it was just the conditions.

TH: But you were really doing it as a favor, because of the heat and the fact that she was sending them back?

AA: And I was in Yosemite and it was easy to do it. I mean, it wasn't a great sacrifice. We had the tanks.

TH: She was having a hard time with them, we know that. And Roy Stryker[3] was very unhappy with it.

AA: Well, I used to plead with Roy to let them [the FSA photographers] come home every so often and do prints so that they'd know what they were getting, get the feel of their own pictures. [He said] "Well, we can print them better than they can." . . . It's the only point of dissension we had. I said, "You're not right. I mean, in photography you want to see what you're getting and if you don't like what you getting you really have to do something about it . . . not just have the photos run through a photo finishing plant. . . ." But Stryker was generous otherwise. . . .

TH: His letters to Dorothea indicated problems. . . .

AA: Well, she was quite difficult to get along with and she probably . . . expressed it.

TH: She had a great habit of going over and around Mr. Stryker which he did not like. It was an administrative game. She would write his superiors. . . .

AA: Yes, I can see that. Well, then after that there was the Office of War Information and we did the shipyards in Berkeley[4] and we did a series of things in San Francisco.

TH: You worked together as friends or you just both got assigned?

AA: Oh, we got along fine. We had a little trouble with the Mormons which I suppose is history now, but she was extremely capable with getting people to do things, getting going through red tape. I was very glad to go along on her coattails on that. . . . She and Paul went to *Life* [magazine] and made the deal. Then Paul went to Salt Lake, and she, too, and [they] said that this was a sociological study . . . an exhibition of life in three villages in southern Utah. And so we got permission, but even then the first week we had trouble. We had been there two weeks and I found out that people had not been told it was a *Life* story. . . . Well, I thought that was pretty unethical, but I was trapped. Well, it came out in *Life* [September 6, 1954], fortunately not as a big story; they had to cut it, but the [Mormon] people were absolutely horrified. Some wanted to sue. I was very embarrassed.

TH: I think Paul brings a different dimension to his view of things, perhaps [more so] than others might because he's interested in gathering information.

AA: Oh, yes. Well, he's one of the greatest farm labor experts anywhere, I guess.

And then we did a job for *Fortune* magazine, agriculture in the valley, the Central Valley. *Fortune* wanted us to go to the big farms where they had all kinds of labor situations. But Dorothea was really adamant about the small farm being the important one. That was Paul's feeling, you see. She would have fights over the telephone with the editor. [They] said, "Dorothea, we've given you a list, the research has been there, that's what we are going to use." . . . That was a strange job. I never had any trouble with the *Fortune* people. . . . I tried to find out what they wanted. I didn't have time for the palavering. You put your own ideas into the pictures. You don't do a lot of yakking about it. But this was really an ideological tournament—the big corporate farms versus the little family farm, and that *Fortune* should favor the latter. Well, if it was some other magazine, but *Fortune* is an industrial-business magazine and they're interested in the big farms. So they were pretty adamant on their side.

TH: How about the Japanese evacuation, Ansel? Did you both work on that independently? The government hired you?

AA: No. She was at work at the time of the evacuation and did some very handsome things. That was a big tragic moment. I didn't have anything to do with that at all. But in Yosemite, after several years, Ralph Merrit came—he was the director of the Manzanar Relocation Center—and I told him, I said, "I'm getting sick and tired of not doing anything." . . . I was too old for the military phase, but I really wanted to, you know, get in. So I spent a lot of time in Yosemite, well, not entertaining, but the troops would come by the thousands and we'd take them out on big tours and make pictures of them, but that was hardly a martial art. Then Ralph Merrit came and I griped, I said, "I'm just not doing anything. We're getting along at the studio all right here. We're doing a little work, but you know. . . ." He said, "Well, I've got a project for you. Come out and shoot my relocation camp." . . . He said, "These people have made a new life for themselves. They've accepted the inevitable. . . . But you have a chance to do a human story about how these people actually triumphed over their circumstance."

So I went down there. It was an amazing experience. Of course, I got them in a very happy mood. You'd say, "Oh, they weren't happy, they were prisoners of war." Well, that'd miss the whole point. The people were glad in their mood and in their acceptance of what they did. Their Japanese gardens, they had beautiful gardens, they had all kinds of cultural efforts, had a fine library . . . a whole little microcosm of a civilization. So they endured that and then they were moved out and they were welcomed all over the country except California. . . .

The whole thing was a nightmare. . . . The recommendation of the military was to take all the Japanese people and get them out. They really expected an attack. . . . But they didn't declare martial law. . . . They could have taken you and me and anybody and moved them all around. National security. But without martial law they took American citizens and literally kidnapped them. . . .

TH: Working with Dorothea as often as you did, . . . did you feel that the fact that she was . . . physically impaired affected her work?

AA: It was hard for her. . . . I always felt that she was amazingly active and when she was immersed in her work she'd really move around. . . . I don't think she'd climb mountains or anything, but I mean, you'd see her up on scaffolds and working very fast with people. But I think it was hard for her to go for any length of time. But the tragic thing was when she had this esophagus trouble. I've seen her in terrible straits at the time, down in Vacaville, down at the San Joaquin Valley and [working on] the Mormon story. She'd really have a terrible time. She couldn't eat. She couldn't swallow. And then they apparently made a mistake. They should have operated at that stage, but they started giving cobalt, other things, and that produced scar tissue and made it much worse. . . . That's what one medical man told me, he said he thought it was a tragedy they didn't catch it earlier. . . .

TH: [Dorothea's] letters to Stryker are almost without any sexual input. I could read the letters and not know if it was a man or a woman. She states simply that she married; she doesn't say "happily I was married" or "my children are doing this or not"; she simply comes on as a photographer among photographers. Did you work with her in the same way?

AA: We got along in a basically fine friendship. I mean, we never had any of *that* kicking. Dorothea was always a little reserved . . . total dedication. Nothing else was going to interfere. And she never had small talk. She could do it for about two minutes and then she'd bring the subject around to something of interest, which I think is good. Small talk is pretty terrible under any conditions. You know how people can just yak and yak and yak. . . . Dorothea had no patience at all with that kind of waste of time and all the people she knew were all dynamic. Of course, she was very . . . very party line and . . . she had very strong sympathies. . . .

TH: Do you think Maynard was behind all that?

AA: Maynard was a very rangy Western, liberal Western. Had no patience at all with any party. . . . He just was intellectually virile on that level. He liked people, liked ideas, but this idea of solidifying into party lines, party concepts, to him [was] just anathema. . . . He was wonderful. He had all the human qualities but the instant you tried to categorize him, Maynard would back off with a kind of scorn, and I think that got Dorothea. . . . But I notice a certain inflexibility in people that it's like an orthodox priest, you know, orthodoxy. It isn't only what you think, but it's the way you think it.

TH: Did you find that came out in Dorothea's work?

AA: Yes, I think in most of the work she gravitated toward some expression that would involve political orientation.

TH: So that somebody who had political interest would recognize it.

AA: Well, that's hard to say. They're not necessarily Commie party pictures, I don't think that. But when she went to Ireland, the group of pictures that she photographed were all of a certain strata. The underdog. The underprivileged. The breadline people. . . . So I think her basic thing in life was to really consider the underdog and of course all the people in our group at that time had a kind of ideal Marxism—didn't really know what the Communist party was—they did later, but . . . you'd go to New York and go to a party on Fifth Avenue, there'd be twenty people at a dinner party, the most elaborate thing you can imagine. You'd see butlers tearing around, New York society [people], and they'd all be talking Commie party line, without knowing what they were talking about.

TH: Do you think Dorothea came to this because of her studio photography . . . and maybe those people turned her off?

AA: No, because she had very dear friends among those people. I think it came from her background in New York. I don't know whether it was ghetto or near ghetto, . . . but it was unpleasant. She probably had experiences that sort of set her, and she had the courage of her convictions, which was wonderful. I admired her for it, because she never compromised. . . . I mean, she wouldn't come forth with unsolicited ideas in an environment she knew would be hostile, but if anybody asked her opinion it wouldn't make a bit of difference who was around. It was always a straightforward answer. In that respect she was absolutely honest and reliable.

About two or three weeks before she died I went over to see her. I took a camera. She didn't look well, but she was still marvelous and sparkling and talking. Her gestures were incredible and I've got five or six series. I don't think they're great shakes as photographs, but they have something of her spirit. Not perfectly sharp, but . . . the older she got the more beautiful she got. Absolute sexless beauty. Rather frightening sometimes. I mean, she became sort of chiseled, sort of a . . . tragic quality, stronger and more luminous.

NOTES

1. Professor of sociology, University of California at Berkeley.

2. Lange photographed in the South from 1936 to 1938, working for the Farm Security Administration (FSA).

3. Head of the FSA.

4. This was actually Richmond, the adjoining city to Berkeley.

Dan Dixon

AFTERWORD

E lizabeth Partridge's introduction to this book has also introduced me to the depth of her feeling about Dorothea Lange. For the first time, I now understand that she was truly a member of our family, related by heart if not by blood. She and I both loved my mother. But while there was much of her that we shared, there was also much of her that we didn't.

I was, after all, Dorothea's son. Over the years, we struggled our way through many different and difficult relationships. She was my demon and my defender, my guide and my goad. I was her adversary and her ally, her critic and her colleague. Even now, almost thirty years after her death, scarcely a day passes when she doesn't enter my thoughts, sometimes with the same uncomfortable questions she used to ask while still alive. "Dan," I hear her say, "Dan, what progress are you making? Why is it taking you so long? What are you doing with your life today?"

No other contributor to this book ever heard Dorothea Lange ask such questions, and no other contributor knew her as well as I did. This, I think, provides me with a special opportunity. And for what it's worth, here is my private and personal experience of Dorothea Lange—Dorothea Lange the friend, the antagonist, the matriarch, the woman.

Genius is mysterious and difficult to describe. But whatever it is, my mother possessed it. She was richly gifted, and in many different ways. You saw it in the rhythm of her movements, felt it in the power of her presence, heard it in the poetry of her speech. Read, for instance, this entry in her journal, written in 1958 during a journey through Asia:

> As we came out of an art store, where we went to find grass cloth, I saw something.
> It had become night, and there was a large, lighted paper lantern, marking an alley.
> The streets were wet from a short rain. There was a tea stall in that alley, behind a
> bright printed half-curtain. And many people there-in. Many legs of young men
> and young women sitting on stools, seen below the curtain. There was a smell of
> food and comfort, and smoking, and relaxation—a kind of pleasure at the day's
> end, and the beginning of the night. I sharply realized how much Tokyo could mean
> to its native people—in this very small scene. All atmosphere. The fellow on the
> stool smoking, half in and half out. This is the Tokyo that I like to remember.

My mother seemed simple, gentle, and direct. She was in truth intricate, subtle, and compelling. Never raising her voice, every gesture a deliberate statement, she dominated everywhere except for behind a camera. There she let her subjects speak for themselves, in their own voices. But with family and friends, she instinctively maneuvered for control. This may make my mother sound disagreeable. She wasn't. Many people loved her, and those who didn't found her intoxicating. More often than not, the force of her will was disguised as persuasion. Even without any calculated design, she could be very seductive. Consider just four examples.

In the early 1920s, while working in the photographic department of a San Francisco stationery store, she was approached by a successful young businessman. He didn't care that she was young and inexperienced, only that she was rare and remarkable. If he put up the money, would she be interested in opening her own portrait studio? She was, and he did, and that studio soon became the city's most fashionable and expensive, capturing what my mother called "the cream of the trade."

Ten years later, during the 1930s, she carried her camera out of the studio and into the streets and fields. There she photographed the victims of the Great Depression. In their shame, anger, and despair, they might have turned their faces away from another photographer, might have even have been hostile and threatening. If they didn't sense her genius, why did they welcome this stranger with the withered leg and the luminous gray eyes? How else was she able to win their trust and confidence so completely?

After World War II, my mother produced occasional picture essays for *Life* and other leading magazines. The editors often flinched from her proposals. They were costly, esoteric, and of little interest to either readers or advertisers. "Three Mormon Towns" wouldn't do anything much to boost circulation, and neither would "The Irish Countryman." Nevertheless, these flinty pragmatists yielded page after precious page to my mother's unlikely projects. She not only managed to get them published, but published in space that she considered suitable and in layouts that she helped supervise. To other photographers, whose stories were less sympathetically handled, this seemed sorcery.

Late in her life, as she became a kind of legend, aspiring photographers bearing portfolios frequently appeared at my mother's door. In time she began to discourage their visits. It was too unsettling, she said. All she did was take them out into the garden and give them a cup of tea and talk with them for an hour or so about the purposes of photography. And then, a few days later, the phone would ring, and there on the end of the line was somebody's wife, perhaps hysterical, complaining that her husband had just decided to quit his job and become a full-time photographer. They were moving to New York, the wife might say, voice choked with reproach. Her whole life had been turned upside down and inside out. And this whole crisis had been caused by a quiet conversation with a little white-haired lady named Dorothea Lange.

Finally, my mother's irresistible influence was felt at home. Her will held our family together. We were a diverse and turbulent bunch—parents and stepparents, children and stepchildren—a profusion of temperaments, talents, rivalries, and relationships. Someone once called us a family jungle, not a family tree. But all of us shared one thing in common. Each of our lives was shaped and colored by my mother's vision of what we were and what we should be. Her genius united us then and continues to unite some of us still. Because of Dorothea Lange, Elizabeth Partridge and I are members of the same family, joined by our memories of that most extraordinary woman.

My mother never described herself as an artist. When she operated her commercial portrait studio, she was a "tradesman." Later on, as a documentary photographer, she became a "witness," an "observer."

For most of my mother's professional life, her mission was to record, not to interpret, the truth. She subordinated herself to her material. She didn't intrude her personality or manipulate the elements. Indeed, unlike most artists, she rigorously resisted the impulse to create. That's why the most compelling feature of her work is its almost painful integrity.

By temperament and instinct, however, an artist is what Dorothea Lange truly was, and I think that there were times when she chafed under the disciplines of her documentary assignments. She must have longed for greater freedom—to state her private feelings, to project her personal vision, to express herself as an artist. This is exactly what she did, though rarely with a camera. Instead she became an artist in the way she crafted her life, fashioned her home, and created her persona.

Her effort began very early. Even as a young girl, growing up in grimy Hoboken, my mother knew that she was uncommon—that she could see. "To you, everything is beautiful," a neighbor once told her. But to Dorothy, her name didn't sound beautiful. It sounded commonplace and conventional. So to everyone but her mother, who continued to call her "Dorothy," she became "Dorothea"—a Dorothea in appearance, as well. Her hair was coiled around her head, then later cropped to her skull. She wore heavy, primitive, exotic jewelry. She smoked when few women dared to, and didn't when many women did. And her clothes weren't clothes; they were costumes.

Some of these garments she designed herself. They were made of coarse white fabrics splashed with vivid embroideries across breast and shoulders, falling in long skirts that curtained her lame leg and twisted foot. She'd been crippled by infantile paralysis when she was seven, but she disguised it so well that some people never realized that she walked with a limp. Dorothy might have surrendered to a disability, but not Dorothea.

What everybody remembers, though, is that her home in Berkeley seemed an enchanted place. Embraced by noble oak trees, it was filled with jars from Korea, tables from Afghanistan, glasses and bowls from Mexico, hangings from Indonesia, hand-hewn farm implements from the Amana society in Iowa, pottery from North Carolina. But most of all, it was filled with Dorothea Lange—her style, her spirit, her taste, her originality, her character. Perhaps that's why some people felt that her home was always changing, while others believed that it always remained the same. Both were true of my mother.

We were never quite prepared for her surprises. Again and again, she startled us with her wit, her generosities, her flashing insights, her impatience, and the intrusions of her will. But there were other things that were entirely predictable. My mother believed in ceremony. Repeated and repeated, routines became rituals. And little by little, year after year, they became articles of faith and acts of devotion. Every Christmas, for a luminous few minutes, our tree glowed with true candlelight. While it lasted, an antique record scratched out the voice of a once famous German diva singing "Silent Night." The eggnog, ripened for weeks in a special stone jug, was dispensed in silver cups. Santa Claus arrived in a rented costume. Led by my mother, hand in hand, the children and grandchildren danced in a circle, and standing in the shadows, watching the ceremony unfold, some of us murmured with discontent.

It was magical, but it was also oppressive. As Elizabeth Partridge also remembers, the pressure to conform was too intense. We wanted Christmas to be *our* Christmas, not just *her* Christmas. We wanted to be ourselves, not simply what she wanted us to be. We wanted to be her family, not her captives. And there were times when she didn't want to be her own captive, either.

In the last two decades of her life, my mother found a release from her own imperatives. It was a crude cabin, leased from the state of California, poised on a cliff at the edge of the Pacific Ocean. Here the family gathered for weekends and holidays, though in a very different spirit than we went to my mother's house in Berkeley. At Steep Ravine, there were no rules or restraints or rituals. We did what we wished, when we wished, as we wished. We were liberated from her strictures and standards, and so was she herself.

This exhilarating sense of freedom was precious to her, and she planned to publish an essay on it. "To tell you the truth," she once said, "I'd rather do this story on the cabin than my big retrospective show at the Museum of Modern Art." She lived to complete the exhibition, but not the essay. However, the photographs she did manage to take were collected into albums and presented as gifts to various members of the family. Here's the inscription she wrote in one of them:

> *"These pictures are of a cabin," says Paulie, and that is exactly right. They are to a cabin, and a life surrounding a cabin—a life independent of "things." There are shells, pebbles, lost socks and wet pants, sands, tides, fire and some sun and stars there. Also fog and wind and weather. I hope to really photograph this, but in the meantime these snapshots are a beginning and will show you that to watch the natural growth of children there, and to see them so happy and free there, is the great joy of—*
>
> *Grandma Dorrie*

She was dying of cancer, and she knew it. When the end came, we placed her ashes in a box on the tides at Steep Ravine. It refused to sink beneath the waves. We stood on the shoreline, watching and waiting. "Look," my brother finally said. "Even now, she's indomitable."

NOTES ON CONTRIBUTORS

ROGER DANIELS, professor of history at the University of Cincinnati, has written widely about Asian Americans and other immigrant groups. His recent books include *Coming to America: A History of Immigration and Ethnicity in American Life* (New York: HarperCollins, 1990) and *Prisoners without Trial: Japanese Americans in World War II* (New York: Hill & Wang, 1993).

DANIEL DIXON is the elder of Dorothea Lange's two sons. He's been a writer and an advertising executive for forty years, and his articles have appeared in many leading magazines and journals. He has also been a political consultant to candidates for governor, mayor, the House of Representatives, the Senate, and president of the United States. He is now a partner in Older & Wiser Ltd., a Los Angeles advertising agency specializing in the mature market, and is working on a book about his father, the artist Maynard Dixon.

THERESE HEYMAN has been senior curator of prints and photographs at the Oakland Museum since 1972. She has organized numerous exhibitions, including a retrospective of Dorothea Lange's photographs, *Celebrating a Collection,* as well as exhibitions of photographs by Richard Misrach and Catherine Wagner. Most recently she completed the book and exhibition, *Seeing Straight,* on the f. 64 group. She is presently on leave from the Oakland Museum to research the photography of Anne Brigman and Ben Shahn.

CLARK KERR, while still a graduate student, served as research assistant to Paul S. Taylor. In 1945, he joined the faculty at the University of California, Berkeley, where he also served as the founding director of its Institute of Industrial Relations until 1952. From 1952 to 1958 he served as chancellor of the Berkeley campus and from 1958 to 1967 as president of the University of California.

LINDA MORRIS is a senior lecturer in English and director of the Women's Studies Program at the University of California, Davis. She received her Ph.D. in English from the University of California, Berkeley. Her recent work includes *Women's Humor in the Age of Gentility: The Life and Works of Frances Miriam Whitcher* (Syracuse University Press, 1992) and *Women's Humor in America: Critical Essays* (Garland Press, 1993).

ELIZABETH PARTRIDGE grew up as part of Dorothea Lange's extended family. In 1974 she was the first person at the University of California, Berkeley, to receive a degree in women's studies. Subsequently she earned a licentiate of acupuncture and a doctorate in Oriental medicine and has been in private practice as an acupuncturist for more than sixteen years. While editing this volume, she co-produced the companion film, *Dorothea Lange: A Visual Life.*

SALLY STEIN is associate professor in the Department of Art History at the University of California, Irvine. She has published a monograph on Farm Security Administration photographer Marion Post Wolcott and is coauthor of *Official Images: New Deal Photography* and *Montage and Modern Life.* Her forthcoming book, *The Rhetoric of the Colorful and the Colorless: American Photography and Material Culture between the Wars,* extends her study of the visual culture of interwar America.